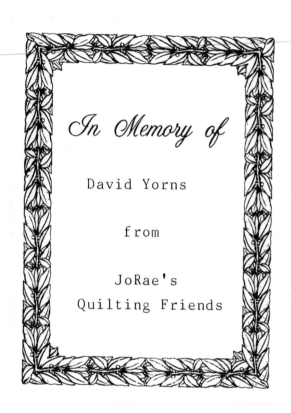

In Memory of

David Yorns

from

JoRae's
Quilting Friends

Jeep

Jim Allen

MBI Publishing Company

DEDICATION

Yet again, to dear Linda.

First published in 2001 by MBI Publishing Company, 729 Prospect Avenue, PO Box 1, Osceola, WI 54020-0001 USA

MBI Publishing Company books are also available at discounts in bulk quantity for industrial or sales-promotional use. For details write to Special Sales Manager at Motorbooks International Wholesalers & Distributors, 729 Prospect Avenue, PO Box 1, Osceola, WI 54020-0001 USA.

Library of Congress Cataloging-in-Publication Data

Allen, Jim.
    Jeep / Jim Allen.
        p. cm.
    Includes index.
    ISBN 0-7603-0797-0 (hc. : alk. paper)
    1. Jeep automobile—History. I. Title.
TL215.J44 A384   2001
629.222'2—dc21   00-066995

On the front cover: A red TJ is at home in the red rocks of Moab, Utah. Moab is one of the premier destinations for Jeepers of all types. During the annual Easter Jeep Safari, you cannot be run over in Moab unless it is by a Jeep.

On the frontispiece: This could be WW II. Herb Huddle's 1944 MB recreates a scene from distant times and hides out in an abandoned barn. The tow bar is an original piece.

On the title page: Two very rare Jeeps in one place. In the foreground is a early 1946 CJ-2A equipped with a Canfield wrecker conversion. With only a few thousand miles on it, the CJ-2A is still wearing its original paint and tires. Perched on the rocks is a restored 1965 CJ-6A Tuxedo Park Mark IV equipped with a half-cab. Both Jeeps are part of the Jim and Peg Marski Jeep collection.

On the back cover: *Top*: The last of the breed. That's what the plaque said on the last of the 1986 model CJs. Many Jeep fans considered this to be the end of an era and the last of the real Jeeps. The last 14 years have proven them wrong. This 1986 model is in Garnet Red and has the original top, a 258ci six, five-speed manual transmission, and air conditioning. This vehicle was found at Collins Brothers Jeep Parts in Wylie, Texas. *Bottom*: A Jeep's life can be easy or hard. In the recreational four-wheel drive world, the latter situation usually applies. Any sort of terrain can be encountered. In this case, Oklahoman Tim Simms, deals with the runoff from a recent downpour. The omnipresent credo in the Jeep world is "be prepared!"

Front Endpaper: Every day was a four-wheeling day in Italy during 1944. With tire chains attached, a jeep slogs along a muddy track with three GIs and an over-capacity load. Just another day in the life of a jeep. *U.S. Army*

Back Endpaper: A Bantam BRC-40 gets a little TLC during maneuvers in Louisiana in 1941. All three pre-standardized units (Ford, Willys, and Bantam) were used for field tests as the U.S. military build up for the inevitable war.

Edited by Amy Glaser
Designed by Tom Heffron
Layout by Katie Sonmor

Printed in Hong Kong

CONTENTS

PREFACE

To enhance your knowledge, understanding and enjoyment of the Jeep world, I welcome you to *Jeep*. Whether you are an admiring fan, a Jeep owner, or a rabid Jeep fanatic, I hope you turn the last page of this book with a big smile on your face.

Although I have written two books and dozens of magazine articles on Jeeps, the research for this book was an eye-opener. I recently discovered aspects to Jeep history that shed new light on the early days. Well, it wasn't really new, just new to me. The material was hiding in plain sight, but much of it has not been published in Jeep histories. If the information was presented, it was usually just hinted at. Some of this "new" information was discovered via a pilgrimage to the National Archives in Washington, D.C., but much of it came from individuals who have spent literally years delving into primary research material and were kind enough to share their documentation with me.

The jeep lore created during World War II was based on an extraordinary American vehicle that, in the hands of some extraordinary Americans, helped win one of the most important struggles of history. It's no wonder that people got excited and from such excitement, legends are born. Legends, as we all know, are a combination of myth and truth. In some cases, deciding what is myth and truth can be difficult.

There are many inaccuracies within the traditional Jeep legend. The inaccuracies evolved from overly eager advertising, wartime propaganda, or people who simply got carried away in moments of excitement and history-making events. Unfortunately, much of this has become "fact" by sheer repetition in the vast amount of published material on the Jeep subject.

The gist of this is especially evident when you read chapters one and two, which provide a slightly different outlook on the story than you might have seen in other books. Less "Win one for the Gipper" and more cold, hard business reality. The winning of jeep contracts was based more on money and politics than on the vehicles themselves. I have tried to present a more sober, nonpartisan view.

Pilot, Prototype, Pre-Standardized, and Production

The terms used for engineering models built prior to production can be confusing, and since a history of Jeep, by necessity, involves a great deal of discussion on these vehicles, the terms are clarified to avoid confusion. A *pilot model* is the first of anything. It essentially defines the concept. A *prototype* refines the pilot model concept. There can be any number of prototypes, each a refinement or upgrade of the pilot model before the vehicle goes into *production*. The production vehicles are stamped out in large numbers to a standardized pattern.

With regard to military designs, which play a large part in Jeep history, *pre-standardized* vehicles may be production vehicles or not, but they are a type the Army has not yet accepted as standard. The pre-standardized jeeps built by Willys, Ford, and Bantam, for example, were production vehicles, albeit low production, so they cannot be accurately described as "prototypes."

ACKNOWLEDGMENTS

Few writers trudge alone into the darkness. In this case, I have a good many Jeep "pioneers" to thank for charting the way. Some are listed in the bibliography, and others are listed below. A few deserve special mention and thanks for help above and beyond the call of duty. This would start with Fred Coldwell, a talented and knowledgeable Jeep expert who willingly shared his time, data, photos, and thoughts. Jim and Peg Marski are well on their way to having the most complete and diverse collection of Jeeps in the world; thanks for enduring the endless photo sessions. To Fred LaPerriere for being one of the most generous military vehicle collectors on the planet. To Jim Gilmore, the foremost expert on Ford-built jeeps, for information and making sure I gave credit where credit is due. To Ron Szymanski, keeper of the Jeep House Museum and holder of the Jeep torch in Toledo, for sharing his extensive knowledge. To Paul and Jane Barry, for sharing knowledge and superb photos. To Pete Sessler for some great photo swaps.

And to:

Bill Ellis, Minneapolis-Moline expert etxraordinaire
Rick Goodell, Holder of the FWD Torch
Herb Huddle, Jeeps, Jeeps and more Jeeps
Lee LaPerriere, Jeep gearhead extraordinaire
Jesse Livingood, for keeping the family business
Bill McCracken, the last Twyford Sales Rep
Todd Paisley, for early Jeeps and exactitude
Jeff Polidoro, for Jeeps in general but mostly for sharing Buddy
Dennis Spence, for vital help with books and literature
Bob Stewart, the world's foremost authority on the Tornado engine
Harold Swartzrock, Minneapolis-Moline preserver
Randy Withrow, Pygmy preserver
George Yokiel, for preserving the last Minneapolis-Moline UTX

CHAPTER 1

1900–1940

SETTING THE STAGE

PREDECESSORS TO THE JEEP

The need for four-wheel drive came on that unheralded day more than a century ago when the first motorist cried "dagnabit" as his wonderful new machine sank to the hubs in mud. A kindly farmer with a team of horses was most often pressed for a rescue, which only added to the ignominy of the situation.

In the turn-of-the-twentieth-century America, fewer than one percent of the nation's roads were paved. Beyond the uncertainties of unproven and cranky machinery, early motorists contended with roads that would deter all but the most hardy of today's four-wheelers. At the dawn of the motorized era, just getting to Auntie Maye's in your newfangled motor car could become an expedition of epic proportions.

Although the name Jeep® has become synonymous with four-wheel drive, the vehicles bearing that name were by no means the first motor vehicles to have that special equipment. There were a large number of worthy four-wheel-drive predecessors dating back to the turn of the century. Some have names that hold almost as much significance as Jeep. No student of Jeep history can call his education complete without knowing about the vehicles, people, and events that set the stage for the Jeep's development.

The Jeffery Quad may be the first four-wheel-drive truck built to Army specifications. Production began in 1914 and many of the first units went to the Army. It served alongside Model Bs in the Punitive Expedition of 1916 and World War I. In 1916, Jeffery was purchased by and absorbed into the Nash organization. The vehicle shown is a restored 1919 Nash-built civilian model that belongs to Quad collector Bruce Rice. The Nash-built trucks differ in several ways from the Jeffery-built varieties, the most noticeable difference being the cast-iron radiator that says "Nash-Quad."

IN THE BEGINNING . . .

You might be surprised to learn that the first known 4x4 was created in 1824. In the early days of steam, Timothy Burstill and John Hill built a steam-powered coach in England, featuring four-wheel drive, front-wheel brakes, and a walking beam engine. The four-wheel-drive feature set this machine apart from the other steam coach experiments of the day. The 7-ton vehicle was tested in 1826 and 1827, but the low power output limited speeds to a mere 4 miles per hour. No problems were reported with the drivetrain, but the Englishmen's steam coach idea died with a bang when the boiler exploded in 1827. The drivetrain was later utilized for a prototype steam locomotive, which also proved to be a failure.

Beyond American Emmett Bandelier's working model and blueprints for a four-wheel-drive steam traction engine in 1883, there wasn't much activity until the dawn of the twentieth century. At that point, exactly who was first with certain advancements in the four-wheel-drive arena is a difficult question to answer. It's clear that a of number four-wheel-drive innovations came at nearly the same time. Some ideas survived and many did not, but at that time, ideas and prototypes were as common as gossip. What follows are

Motivations for the perfection of four-wheel drive were situations like this. When less than one percent of the nation's roads were paved at the turn of the century, this was a common occurrence. This photo was taken around 1910 and the car was attempting to win a $1,000 prize by following the FWD Battleship four-wheel-drive touring car cross-country. Here's photographic proof that this particular car didn't make it. *FWD*

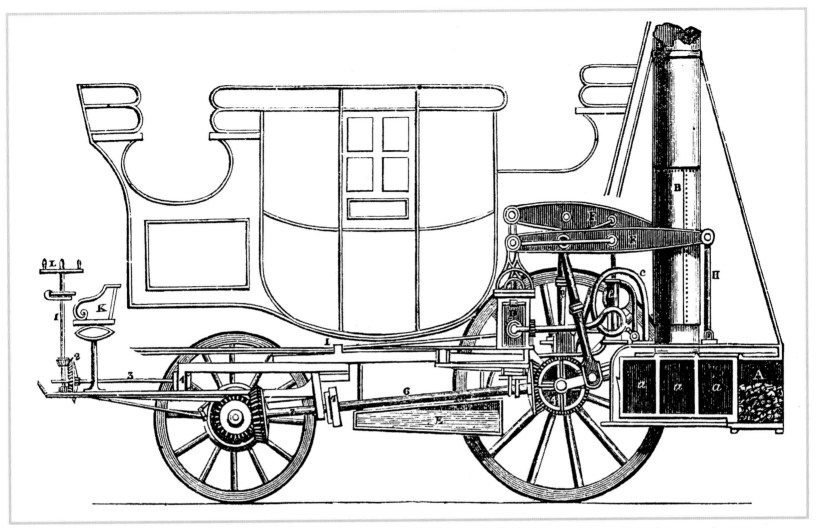

The Burstill and Hill steam car of 1824 is most likely the first four-wheel-drive ever built. Power from the walking beam engine was delivered directly to the rear axle and transmitted to the front via two sets of bevel gears on a shaft. The drive system worked well, but not the boiler; it exploded in 1827.

some of the highlights, but by no means the full measure, of four-wheel-drive development in the early part of the twentieth century.

Twyford

Robert E. Twyford formed the Twyford Motor Vehicle Company in Pittsburgh, Pennsylvania, in 1899, and received a patent for a four-wheel-drive system in 1900. At least one, and possibly three, vehicles were built up to 1902. In 1904, Twyford reestablished the company in Brookville, Pennsylvania, with the help of assorted investors from that town. The Twyford featured a rear-mounted 9-horsepower, two-cylinder Sintz valveless engine, best known at the time as a marine power plant. The front driving axle was of the platform type (the entire axle pivoted in the center like a wagon). A unique feature was the gear-driven power-steering system. Twyfords were offered as touring cars, stanhopes, runabouts, express, and

delivery vehicles. Although the company built a handful of cars through 1907, it went out of business that year. After moving to Texas, Twyford made another try at car building in 1911 under the Brandon nameplate, but that company went into receivership in 1912.

Cotta

Charles Cotta of Rockford, Illinois, developed a steam-powered touring car in 1900 that featured a chain-drive four-wheel-drive system. It's uncertain how many units were built, but Cotta advertised the cars through 1902 in magazines like the *Cycle and Automobile Trade Journal*. The *Cottamobile* featured platform steering and a complicated chain-drive setup. In 1903, Cotta sold the designs and patents to the Milwaukee Four Wheel Drive Wagon Company, which reputedly built small numbers of 4x4

cars and trucks up to 1907. Cotta went on to design and manufacture truck transmissions in the following years.

Porsche

About the same time America was struggling with four-wheel-drive ideas, Ferdinand Porsche, originator of the Volkswagen, was an unknown 25-year-old engineer in Europe. When he was contracted to design an electric vehicle for the Lohner Electric Car Company in Vienna, Austria, he came up with a 4x4 that had an electric motor in each wheel hub. After some promising test results, the vehicle was rebuilt to set a world speed record with the addition of extra batteries. The *La Toujours Contente*, as it was named, could only

A 1905 JEEP?

Research may yield many odd connections to a story. One such connection to the Jeep story came in the form of a proposal from 1905 that was found at the National Archives. Capt. William A. Phillips, from the 10th U.S. Infantry stationed at Fort Lawton, Washington, wrote a 15-page proposal outlining the current state of the automobile art and ways this new technology could benefit the Army. He went on to urge the testing of current vehicles to develop a database of knowledge, and to begin building lists of standards and specifications for military vehicles.

He detailed the particular needs of a military vehicle quite astutely for his time, especially considering the lack of experience and testing in the automobile area. Some of the needs Phillips included in his proposal were high clearance for obstacles like stumps and rutted roads, deep water fording, low gearing for climbing hills and obstacles, a power takeoff-driven drum winch for self-recovery, and four-wheel drive to enable the vehicle to surmount the hostile terrain often encountered on the battlefield.

Phillips projected that this machine should have 8-inch-wide flotation tires, and be able to attain a maximum speed of at least 15 miles per hour, but also be able to slog as slowly as one mile per hour in hard terrain. It should also be equipped with a winch and an electrical dynamo to operate a wireless telegraph. He proposed using the 4x4s as staff cars, bridge

building outfits, personnel carriers, ambulances, artillery prime movers, fuel tankers, machine shops, and even as machine gun carriers.

Phillips completed his proposal by stating, "Let us put the prejudice aside and give this new invention, the automobile, a fair opportunity to show what it can do as a factor in the art and science of war." As you read the early parts of this book that involve military development and use of the military jeep, it becomes clear how farsighted this unknown officer was for his time.

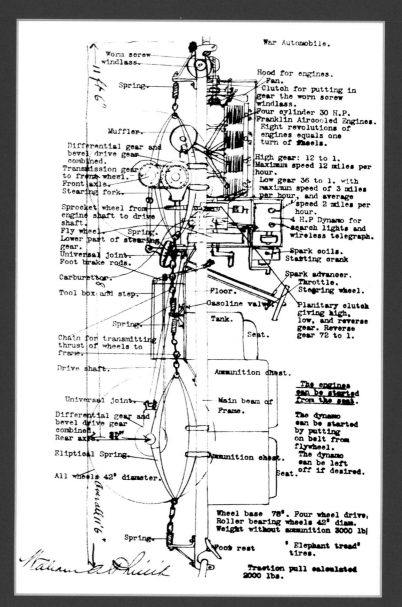

If you look through Phillip's specifications for the War Automobile, take note of how many similarities there are with the later jeep. Besides the four-wheel drive and four-cylinder engine, the basic dimensions and capacities are similar. The comparisons can be seen in the following chart:

	WWII JEEP	WAR AUTOMOBILE
Wheelbase	80 in	78 in
Overall Length	132.75 in	138 in
Engine	4-cyl, 60hp, water-cooled	4-cyl, 30hp, air-cooled
Curb Weight	2,415 lbs	3,000 lbs
Lowest O/A Gear Ratio	24.6:1 forward	36:1 forward
	34.1:1 reverse	72:1 reverse
Traction Pull	1,930 lbs	2,000 lbs

The Duplex Model B was built, on and off, from 1909 to 1914. It was rated for a 2,500-pound load and was powered by a 196-ci, two-cylinder, horizontally opposed engine that cranked out 20 horsepower from a 5-inch bore and stroke. It had a two-speed planetary transmission, single-speed transfer case, and spur and rig gear drive at the wheels. All the early Duplex trucks were relatively successful and served in World War I. The company went on to specialize in large all-wheel-drive trucks.

manage a 50 miles-per-hour maximum speed, 15.7 miles per hour short of the world speed record at the time.

Spyker

The Spyker Carriage Works in Holland built a four-wheel-drive race car in 1903 that holds the honor of being first four-wheel-drive design to feature a steerable front axle. Although the system was built primarily for road holding, the layout matches the general setup of today. The Spyker also holds the record for the first six-cylinder inline engine: a massive 537-cubic-inch, 60-horsepower unit. Three or four other 4x4 cars were produced by Spyker. The first car was successfully raced and did especially well in bad weather.

Van Winkle

Meanwhile, back in the States, Charles Van Winkle, of San Joaquin, California, built and patented a four-wheel-drive system in 1905. His four-wheel-drive concept utilized a single drive shaft that connected the front and rear axles and was installed on a touring car chassis. Van Winkle sold the patents to the newly formed Stockton Four Drive Auto Company in Stockton, California, but the idea went nowhere. Van Winkle later built two-wheel-drive trucks in 1913 and 1914 at Atlanta, Georgia. A later version of Van Winkle's system appeared in the short-lived Twin Cities four-wheel-drive truck of 1917.

Couple Gear

The Couple Gear Freight Wheel Company, of Grand Rapids, Michigan, began building four-wheel-drive electric trucks in 1906 that, like Porsche's machine, had electric motors in each hub. The Couple Gear trucks were built mainly for city use and had a steering system that allowed the front and rear wheels to be independently operated. The trucks were capable of moving sideways with both sets of wheels turned in the same direction. Some Couple Gear trucks were run only by battery and others were also fitted with a gas-powered generator to travel longer distances.

American

Also in 1906, the American Motor Truck Company built its first four-wheel-drive, four-wheel-steer chain-drive truck. A small number of trucks in the 1- to 10-ton range were built through 1912. One prototype, thought to be the original, is known to have survived in a private collection. The vehicles were platform steer units, but like most four-wheel-steer trucks, they had the annoying habit of running one end into the curb when pulling away.

Duplex

Charlotte, Michigan, was the home of the Duplex Power Car Company. Some sources list 1907 as the founding year, but period publications dispute that date. For example, the July 1, 1909, edition of *Motor World*

announced that Duplex had just produced its first 14-horsepower, four-wheel-drive wagon. After some rocky times, Duplex remained a player in the big all-wheel-drive truck market well into the 1960s. A portion of Duplex remains in business in Ohio under the Simon-Duplex nameplate, and produces fire-fighting equipment and specialty truck chassis.

FWD: THE FOUR-WHEEL-DRIVE BREAKTHROUGH

The development of a steerable front axle in America opened the door to more practical four-wheel drives. Otto Zachow, a machinist from Wisconsin, had the honor of patenting the first American steerable front driving axle in 1908. His story is probably the most famous to come from the early 4x4 pioneers. Along with partner William Besserdich, Zachow had gone into the automobile sales and repair business in 1905. When their first automobile arrived in February 1906, it created enough of a sensation in their hometown of Clintonville that three more vehicles were sold before the end of summer.

Life with the automobile, though by no means easy in those days, was at least predictably difficult until bad weather and muddy roads came with the change of the seasons. From the fall of 1906 to the spring of 1907, Zachow's poor Reo was stranded in mud more often than not. Zachow and the other Clintonville motorists became quite adept at recovery, but an accidental "tour" of a ravine gave Zachow the idea for a four-wheel-drive car.

Careless driving had put Zachow off the road on a hillside in the nearby town of Appleton. Seeing flat ground at the bottom of the slope, Zachow reckoned he had a better chance of getting back on the road by going the rest of the way down the ravine to get a running start. What he hadn't noticed was the steep bank at the bottom.

When Zachow got the Reo turned around, he found that the front wheels merely dug into the steep bank and the rear wheels spun. After thinking for a few moments, he turned the Reo around and pulled the vehicle up the bank using the rear wheels. On the way home, his mind began to germinate an

The FWD Auto Company's "Battleship" was completed in 1909 and was the pilot model for a small number of 4x4 touring cars built by that company to 1912. It was used as a sales tool and traveled to fairs and events to offer a $1,000 prize to the owner of any car that could follow it for 15 minutes cross-country. It had a 423-ci, 45-horsepower engine, three-speed transmission, and a single-speed, chain-drive transfer case. To celebrate the company's 50th anniversary in 1960, the Battleship made a round-the-country tour, stopping in Hollywood for a drag race against Jack Benny's 1914 Maxwell down Sunset Boulevard. Even with Rochester driving, the Maxwell was no match for the Battleship. The Battleship is in running condition at the FWD Museum in Pioneer Park, located in Clintonville, Wisconsin.

idea, and a short while later, he said to Besserdich, "Whoever heard of a mule who walked on just two legs!" This observation, along with an article in *Scientific American,* set the Wisconsin machinists to work designing a driving front axle. In just a few years, Zachow's patent helped create the Badger Four Wheel Drive Auto Company, known after 1910 as the Four-wheel Drive Auto Company, and later, simply as FWD.

Zachow and Besserdich's first prototype made its debut in 1908 and used a four-wheel-drive layout similar to what is still used today. It was powered by an unreliable cross-compound steam engine, a feature that was dropped quickly. Besides the steam engine, the Badger had a three-speed gearbox, a single-speed, full-time, chain-drive transfer case, and a fairly standard rear differential. It was also minus a body and used a dry goods box for

a seat. The front axle, with its double "Y" driving yokes for steering while transmitting power, is what made the unit special.

After tests in late 1908, the Badger went into the shop for refinement. It emerged in mid-1909 with a 392-ci Continental engine and a stunning red touring car body. In further tests, the car proved to be the pinnacle of performance. It was nicknamed the "Battleship," because nothing could stop it. It was taken to fairs and shows where a $1,000 prize was offered to any car that could follow it cross country for 15 minutes. By 1910, the Battleship had racked up nearly 10,000 miles and bested at least 116 cars in that year alone.

Zachow and Besserdich soon acquired business expertise in the person of local lawyer Walter Olen. Olen soon became the guiding force and remained in control for many years. His stern but able guidance soon put

FWD at the top of the heavy-duty all-wheel-drive truck market. Zachow and Besserdich both left the company early on, Zachow to a quiet life of tinkering and Besserdich to co-found another big-truck all-wheel-drive milestone company named Oshkosh.

DIRECT INFLUENCES

A large number of vehicles could be considered a direct influence on the development of the Jeep. The following are the heavy hitters in that category for reasons that are clear. In some cases, there is even a direct lineage from a corporate standpoint. In others, it was simply a pivotal development that broke new ground or inspired the next generation of inventors and ultimately the Jeep.

This is the Army's first 4x4 truck as it appeared in late January 1912, just before it was loaded on a train for delivery to Washington, D.C. This vehicle cost the taxpayers $1,904. The rig started as an four-wheel-drive Touring Car, but with the addition of a cargo box taken from an Army escort wagon, it became a one-ton truck known as the "Scout Car." This car began the long process of proving the value of all-wheel drive in military operations over two-wheel-drive vehicles and horses.

The four-wheel-drive Scout Car participated in the U.S. Army's first major cross-country test of motor vehicles from February 8 to March 28, 1912. The 1,509-mile winter trip tested all four of the trucks, literally, to the breaking point. The four-wheel drive was the only 4x4 in the bunch and often did double duty by scouting the road ahead or towing the other vehicles out of the mud. It's shown here upon its arrival in Atlanta on March 10, 1912. Driver-mechanic Jimmie Gaughan is behind the wheel; Capt. Alexander E. Williams, U.S. Army, Officer in Charge of the test, is in the long coat; and Frank Dorn, four-wheel drive test driver, is at the far right.

1911: FWD Scout Car

This one-off adaptation of an FWD Touring Car was the U.S. Army's first four-wheel-drive vehicle, and it persuaded the first of many Army motor officers that four-wheel drive was the only way to go. In late 1911, sales of the Four Wheel Drive Auto Company's four-wheel-drive touring cars was slow. FWD had already decided to jump into truck production when management heard of a U.S. Army-sponsored cross-country test. It enticed the officer in charge, Capt. Alexander E. Williams, into a factory visit. When he saw what the FWD cars could do, he recommended the purchase of one for tests.

The Army bit, and for $1,904, a stripped-down chassis was delivered on January 25, 1912, for use in the upcoming Army tests. By early February, an escort wagon cargo box had been added and the touring car became a 1-ton truck. From February 8 to March 28, 1912, the "Scout Car," as it came to

The four-wheel-drive Model B 3-ton truck became a mainstay of the U.S. Army surrounding the time of World War I. It also was a commercial success starting with production from 1912 to well into the 1930s. Shown here is a model M-1917 with the ammunition body, painted in original World War I camouflage.

be known, endured 1,500 miles of muddy and rough roads from Washington, D.C., to Fort Benjamin Harrison, Indiana. Carrying a 2,000-pound simulated payload, plus food, fuel, and spare parts, the Scout Car was often called upon to tow or drag the other three test trucks (all large 1 1/2 ton 4x2s) over the rougher parts of the trail. It suffered several breakdowns, but considering its original designed purpose, the ersatz truck held up well.

In June 1912, the Scout Car participated in the first motorized Army maneuvers to involve motor trucks. Later that year, it was used in a 150-mile "speed run" from Fort Leonard Wood, Missouri, to Fort Riley, Kansas, a feat it performed in eight hours. The Scout Car was placed under Signal Corps control for use at the Army Aviation School in San Diego, California, and from there its ultimate fate is unknown.

1912–1919: FWD Model B Trucks

The Model B 3-ton truck was one of the first truly successful, high-volume production all-wheel-drive trucks. Development started in late 1911, along with a 1 1/2-ton truck. Prototypes of each were finished just in time for use in the Army's first test of motor trucks on field maneuvers in 1912. A Provisional Regiment of infantry was marched from Dubuque, Iowa, to Sparta, Wisconsin, and the trucks were detailed to make daily supply runs over long distances on roads that ran the gamut from O.K. to impossible. A total of 12 trucks were used, and many were leased from the manufacturers for that specific purpose. The old Scout Car, the two FWD trucks and a Kato were the only four-wheel drives.

The two FWD trucks earned very high marks for durability and off-highway performance. Both models went into production, though neither saw extensive

The first four-wheel-drive vehicle to show true jeeplike traits was the Livingood conversion of the Model T from the J. L. Livingood Company. Light and compact, it embodied everything the jeep later became. It seems a miracle that the Army did not get wind of this inexpensive conversion and test or use it. The conversions were offered from 1914 through 1928, and in limited numbers after that time. In fact, you can still buy a conversion from the inventor's son.

military use in the early years due to FWD's unwillingness to adopt Army specifications. Large numbers of Model B trucks did, however, serve exceptionally well in the 1916 Punitive Expedition to Mexico as well as in World War I. About 16,000 were built for the Great War, and some went to the British and French armies, but most were used by the U.S. Army. The Model B 3-ton established FWD's reputation as a major truck builder. The Model B became one of the company's mainstays, staying in production well into the 1930s. FWD remains in business in Clintonville, Wisconsin.

1914–1919: Jeffery (Nash) Quad Trucks

This four-wheel-drive, four-wheel-steer truck has technical, corporate, and military ties to the Jeep. The Quad project was started by the Thomas B. Jeffery Company, of Kenosha, Wisconsin. It made its debut in September 1913 in direct response to Jeffery getting an inside tip about a possible government request for bids on a new all-wheel-drive military truck. The specifications that the Army later drew up and offered for general bids almost exactly matched those of the Quad. This testified to the truck's favorable impact on the Army and some good lobbying by Mr. A. Cranston, Jeffery's Washington representative.

The Quad was purchased in large numbers by the U.S. military starting in 1915. The Quad was a big participant in the dash across the Mexican border in pursuit of Pancho Villa during the 1916 Punitive Expedition. In late 1916, the Thomas B. Jeffery Company was sold to Charles Nash, and the Quad became a part of the Nash lineup. With several upgrades, it

Often inaccurately called the "Granddaddy" of the jeep, the Marmon-Herrington LD-1 was nevertheless a big link in the chain of events leading up to the jeep. M-H opened the doors to a light-duty 4x4 movement by building this 4x4 conversion of a half-ton Ford truck in 1936. Although it was originally intended for the Belgian government, the conversions were successfully tested by the Army and used prior to the rearmament days of 1939–1941.

entered service with American Forces in World War I. Around 23,000 Quads were built and proved to be popular and reliable military trucks. They saw military service into the 1920s.

The corporate connection to Jeep comes from the Nash angle. In the 1950s, Nash became part of American Motors, and American Motors owned the Jeep line from 1970 to 1987. Another tie to Jeep is the name Quad. The first Willys prototype was also named Quad. The Nash Quad's four-wheel steering inspired generations of military men to request this feature in military rigs. The Jeep was no exception, and a great deal of experimentation was done on four-wheel steering during its development. The Quad was also the first 4x4 to offer locking differentials in the axles. Civilian Quads were built up to 1928.

1914–1928: Livingood 4x4 Conversion

In my opinion, the Livingood four-wheel-drive conversion of the Model T Ford was the earliest example of the concept that the Jeep later embodied so well. Beginning in 1914, the J. L. Livingood Company, of New Virginia, Iowa, offered a four-wheel-drive conversion kit for Model T Fords. The combination of a lightweight, compact vehicle with all-wheel-drive traction was suitable for many light infantry support and reconnaissance roles. It's unclear why the Livingood was never tested by the Army. The conversion was not widely known, but it certainly wasn't obscure, given the number of surviving adver-

tisements. Livingood lasted as a company through 1928 but the proprietor, Jesse Livingood, experimented with conversions to Model A Fords and Chevrolets into the 1930s.

1934: Dodge K-39-X-4USA

The 1934 Dodge 1 1/2 tons offered a cost-effective four-wheel-drive truck that the Army purchased in relatively large numbers. What was pivotal about the Dodge is that it had a part-time transfer case, the first such application in a production vehicle. Prior to that, trucks used a full-time setup with a center differential. This led to traction problems when a center differential lock was not installed, and increased mileage, tire wear, and steering problems without a center differential. The part-time T-case disconnected the front axle and turned the truck into a 4x2. Part-time transfer cases are the norm today, but this Dodge, and the others that followed through the 1930s, were a big deal in their day.

1936: Marmon-Herrington

This Indianapolis, Indiana-based company began business in 1931. It produced a line of vehicles that are considered a milestone in the development of the light-duty 4x4, including the jeep. To begin the company, Walter C. Marmon brought cash and financial acumen while Col. Arthur W. Herrington (Ret.) brought vast technical experience from years of military all-wheel-drive research and testing. Herrington was one of the major players in the development of the Army's all-wheel-drive fleet.

According to market demand, Marmon-Herrington (M-H) focused on larger trucks, first with a 4x4 truck it built from the ground up, and later with Ford trucks converted to four-wheel drive. The light-duty breakthrough came in July 1936, when a special request from the Belgian government encouraged M-H to convert a 1936 Ford half-ton pickup to all-wheel drive. The V8-powered truck was further militarized by the removal of the cab and the installation of a canvas cover. The truck was overwhelmingly successful, both in terms of performance and cost effectiveness. It may well have been the best-performing off-highway vehicle on the planet in its narrow time frame.

It was found that the M-H truck could carry a heavy weapons squad or tow light artillery across extremely rough ground. The beauty was that, aside from the four-wheel-drive hardware, the truck was essentially good ol' Ford stuff. The Belgian government and the U.S. Army both placed an order for the half-ton M-H trucks. These trucks were tested in every conceivable role and found wanting only in size. While the half- and three-quarter-ton trucks had a firm place in Army livery, a small, light, nimble recon car was desperately needed as well.

1937: The Bellyflopper

In the midst of all the other ideas being pursued simultaneously by commercial elements, the Army did some experimentation on its own. One such project began in 1936 at Fort Benning, Georgia. The need for a light weapons carrier for close infantry support was regarded as a high priority by Infantry officers. To that end, Brig. Gen. Walter C. Short, assistant commander of the

Before and during World War I, light motor transport duties were handled by ordinary 4x2 cars. In this 1917 shot, a Dodge Brothers touring car undergoes a fording test and manages not to get stuck.

Infantry shoot at Benning, assigned Capt. Robert C. Howie and M. Sgt. M. C. Wiley to build a prototype machine gun carrier. With a whopping budget of $500 (reputedly liberated from another department's funds), Howie and Wiley began building a new idea in close infantry support.

What emerged in April 1937 was the Howie-Wiley machine gun carrier, commonly known as the "Bellyflopper." This term came from the noticeable characteristic of the carrier's two-man crew driving and firing in the prone position. The Bellyflopper was little more than a steel plate to which a pair of axles (one driving, one steering) and an engine had been attached. There was no suspension.

It's often said that the simplest ideas are the most successful. The Bellyflopper exceeded all expectations as a machine gun carrier. At only 1,015 pounds, it could be lifted in and out of a light truck by a handful of men. It could scoot around the battlefield at almost 30 miles per hour, powered by a 1937 46-ci, 20-horsepower Bantam engine. It could mount a .30 Browning heavy machine gun and carry 1,500 rounds of ammo. It had an extremely low 33-inch silhouette and was easily hidden. The Bellyflopper could be regarded as the 1930s equivalent of a stealth ground vehicle. To paraphrase the immortal Mohammed Ali, the Bellyflopper could scoot like a cockroach and sting like a bee. A low ground clearance and limited 4x2 traction were the major complaints, but many of the characteristics embodied in the Bellyflopper found their way into the later quarter-ton.

The Dodge VC series half-ton trucks that made their debut late in 1939 were also an inspiration to the creators of the jeep. In fact, the Command Car versions were commonly called jeeps by the troops well before the quarter-ton even existed.

1940: Dodge VC Trucks

Although Marmon-Herrington was the first off the mark with a production light-duty 4x4 for military use, Dodge carried the concept to new heights. Its VC series trucks brought the company a major military contract for half-ton trucks and later for the ubiquitous 3/4 ton. The VC trucks began a dynasty in military transport that lasted nearly 30 years.

The VCs were an adaptation of the civilian line of Dodge trucks. Take a one-ton Dodge commercial chassis, derate it to a half-ton capacity for extreme military use, strip it of all unnecessary body parts, add four-wheel drive and military accoutrements and you have the formula for a successful army truck. What is most interesting is that the command car version, the Dodge VC-1, was often called "Jeep" by GIs for reasons that will be explained in chapter 9.

DEFINING THE NEED

TURNING A CONCEPT INTO A REALITY

Through the early years of motor vehicles, four-wheel drive was an expensive option. Any motor vehicle so equipped was at least twice the cost of a similar 4x2. In those days, you could buy a Duesenberg for the price of a four-wheel-drive truck. Getting stuck was much less expensive. Because four-wheel drive was so expensive, its limited marketability was only in the civilian commercial arena, primarily with buyers of larger trucks. These cost and marketability issues slowed down the development of four-wheel-drive trucks, especially those in the light-duty realm. The military was one exception.

The 1916 Punitive Expedition to Mexico was the first time motor trucks were used in an American campaign. World War I proved the value of all-wheel-drive motor vehicles on the battlefield, but there was still a great resistance among military hierarchy. To these old-fashioned officers, the army boot and the horse were still the king and queen of battlefield transport. Despite these holdouts, the military became one of the major driving forces in the perfection of four-wheel-drive technology.

The BRC-40 was Bantam's last gasp as a quarter-ton builder. Light and nimble, the BRC was reputed to be the nicest driving of the three pre-standardized jeeps. Just over 2,600 units were built in 1941. The Bantams are the second most common of the remaining pre-standardized jeeps. This early BRC-40 was restored by Ken Hake, the man who has restored more pre-standardized jeeps than anyone.

U p through World War I, American light transport consisted of motorcycles, two-wheel-drive civilian cars, and light trucks. Ford Model Ts and Dodge Brothers touring cars and pickups were the most common light-duty models. Two-wheel drive hampered their usefulness, but through the 1920s and early 1930s, motor transport pundits explored the light reconnaissance idea while fighting minuscule budgets, the backwards thinking of high-ranking officers, and a large technology gap. Several low-cost rough-ground performance improvement ideas were tried, and most involved a stripped-down 4x2 automobile chassis fitted with flotation tires. Total satisfaction in cross-country performance was not achieved, but several types were adopted in limited numbers for Army use.

The motorcycle, with or without a sidecar, had long been the primary light reconnaissance and messenger vehicle of the ground forces, but it was less than satisfactory. Only a very skilled rider could go cross-country on an early motorcycle. They were also largely unreliable and the cargo/weapons capacity was almost nil. Injuries and accidents were common among the riders. The motorcycle had continued in the Army because it was all it had in the line of light recon vehicles.

This contraption has a direct connection to the jeep from a conceptual and corporate standpoint. Few pictures of this modified 1933 American Austin car remain. The Army bought this unit in 1934 and modified it for cross country use. By stripping it to bare bones and adding flotation tires, the Army was able to improve cross-country performance somewhat. The T1E1 triple .30-caliber anti-aircraft gun mount gave the little Austin a healthy sting. Experiments like this, generally tested on a budget, slowly gave the Army a picture of the vehicle the jeep ultimately became.

as the American Austin Car Company of Butler, Pennsylvania. The first American Austins were essentially British Austins built under license and "Americanized" by the addition of left-hand steering. After a novelty sales spurt that lasted a year, these small but solid cars were more or less snubbed by the American public.

The company went into receivership in 1932 but was saved by the efforts of Roy Evans, a dynamic young Florida car salesman. Evans soon found himself hired as the top dog at American Austin and managed to keep the company barely afloat until the middle of 1934, when the inevitable bankruptcy was filed. Evans was then able to procure the company for a mere $5,000 in cash and the assumption of debts. Evans and American Austin president Francis Fenn put the lineup through a major facelift, and gave the cars a stylish new look and a big increase in power. In January 1938, with a new identity, the American Bantam Car Company presented its new cars to the public.

The public didn't beat down the doors at Bantam dealerships, but enough were sold to keep the company operating on a shoestring. The money finally ran out in 1940, when only a handful of cars were produced and the factory staff was reduced to 15 people, including executives. It was at this point the U.S. Army and Bantam successfully came together to start the jeep wheels turning.

The year 1940 was not the first time American Austin/Bantam had made a play for a government contract. In 1933, American Austin submitted a pickup for tests at Fort Benning, Georgia, as a cross-country or scout car. The service liked the compact size and fuel economy (around 50 miles per gallon) but was not impressed with its cross-country performance or durability. Still, the Army liked it enough to buy one (for a whopping $286.75) strip it to bare bones, install a set of flotation tires, and test it some more. Cross-country ability improved somewhat, but the durability did not.

In 1938, the company, now under the Bantam nameplate, made another play by supplying three vehicles to the Army for tests at Fort Benning, Georgia, Fort Riley, Kansas, and Camp Holabird, Maryland. The new Bantams were much improved over the old ones from a reliability standpoint, but were still hampered in the dirt by two-wheel drive. In 1939, more Bantam cars were tested by the Pennsylvania National Guard during its annual maneuvers. Another generally favorable report got Bantam's military sales representative, Charles Payne, a foot in the door. Meetings with officers from the Chiefs of Infantry and Cavalry produced an idea for a light reconnaissance car based on the Bantam chassis. The response was promising. The Ordnance Technical Committee, constituted of officers from all

Chain of Events

There are many links in the chain of events that led to the development of the quarter-ton 4x4 we now call the Jeep. The first fact Jeep history students need to remember is that no one person or company "invented" the quarter-ton 4x4. The concept evolved from evaluating many years of military operational necessities and combining it with the technology available at the moment. It boils down to this: the United States Army invented the jeep by producing a list of specifications and design parameters for the manufacturers to build a vehicle around.

The companies responding to the 1940 government call for bids each contributed a great deal of unique insight and expertise to the project. Participants later in the program helped refine the jeep. All companies contributed vital elements to the vehicle that became the standard quarter-ton. Some of those contributions have been overshadowed by revisionist histories done in the 1940s and 1950s but today, the work of Bantam, Willys-Overland, and Ford have generally been given proper credit by historians.

American Bantam Car Company

Bantam was one of the few compact car specialists existing in the United States through the 1930s and 1940s. The company began business in 1929

"OLD NUMBER ONE" SCRAPBOOK

The big day! This photo was taken just before the world's first quarter-ton was delivered. Harold Crist is behind the wheel, with Frances Fenn in the passenger seat and Karl Probst leaning on the spare tire.

Complete with the famous "headslapper" top, the Bantam Reconnaissance Car was photographed on October 2, 1940, during an early point in Army tests.

The little Bantam must have had as much time hauling "suits" and "brass" around for photo ops as it did in tests. Some now-forgotten "suit" gets the ride of his life in October 1940.

This distinctive front end appeared only once. The fenders, cowl, and hood came from a Bantam car.

The Bantam Pilot model is the first quarter-ton. As such, it has attracted a great deal of attention, as many firstborns do. Unfortunately it did not survive to claim its rightful seat on the throne of history. It barely survived five months and was damaged in a collision with a utility truck and never was repaired.

The prototype Bantam BRC-60 models were much like the pilot, but featured a more military set of front fenders. This is Bantam number 007, now owned by the Smithsonian Institution.

The Pygmy is shown here in recent times. The well-used Ford pilot was used for World War II ~~promotions~~ during the war and later lived at the Henry Ford museum until the mid-1980s. A sale put the unit in private hands, and soon the Alabama Center for Military History, currently under construction in Huntsville, Alabama, will be displaying this historic jeep. *Alabama Center for Military History*

branches of the Army, assigned a technical subcommittee to investigate the Bantam facility.

Over a two-day period in June 1940, the subcommittee, including Maj. Robert G. Howie of Bellyflopper fame, viewed the factory and tested a number of Bantam car variations. The time spent testing and discussing ideas was valuable and put the Bantam reconnaissance car onto a new track by adding four-wheel drive to the concept.

Howie remained at Bantam for another week after the rest of the subcommittee departed to flesh out rough plans and specifications for a totally new military vehicle. Spicer was consulted about the possibility of building a light-duty front-driving axle and a compact two-speed transfer case. The nine-day engineering "jam session" proved fruitful, and the Army's requirements for a light reconnaissance car were largely based on Howie's intimate knowledge of Army operational needs and Bantam's experience building compact cars.

After refinement by Army engineers, technical specifications for the new 4x4 were released, but to Bantam's surprise and chagrin, they were also sent to 134 other manufacturers for bids. Bantam was miffed, but it rallied and quickly responded, knowing the fate of the company rested on this contract.

When the invitation to bid was received at Bantam, it echoed through the empty halls of the plant. Bantam needed a chief engineer/designer in a hurry and a call went out to Karl K. Probst, a reliable freelance engineer known to Bantam confidants. He was offered a fantastic "deal" to work his tail off for a chance at

very little money. He reluctantly agreed on July 17, leaving just five days to come up with a tentative design and work out the costs in order to make a bid. Fortunately, Probst had a fine core group of gearheads at Bantam to work with, but the five days were grueling.

In a miracle of concentration and endless hours, he put together a comprehensive design, fudging only with the weight. Probst saw right off that the 1,275-pound weight limit was impossible. In the end, the 1,850-pound estimated weight was changed to 1,300 pounds and engineers hoped to skin some weight off in production.

Quad! It's the name of a vehicle that was made famous in World War I, and the name of the Willys-Overland entry into the 1940–1941 battle for the quarter-ton contracts. The Quad did indeed evolve into a legendary vehicle but not under that name. The Willys pilot model, along with its four-wheel-steer brother, was successfully tested in late 1940 and early 1941, but it was not initially accepted because it was 360 pounds overweight.

Willys-Overland

Willys-Overland (W-O) began under the energetic and dynamic leadership of John North Willys. Willys had taken over the nearly defunct Overland Car Company in the dark days of 1907, purchased it in 1908 and by 1915, had turned W-O into the world's second largest car builder. By 1917, the Willys Corporation, which began as a holding company for Willys-Overland, also owned the Curtiss Aeroplane and Motor Corporation and the Moline Plow Company (later known as Minneapolis Moline).

A slump after World War I brought the Willys financial empire to its knees and J. N. Willys began to divest of many holdings, keeping Willys-Overland as his last holdout. By 1921, W-O was more than $17,000,000

This derelict has earned the right to be in this book by its remarkable survival. This is *the* original Budd-bodied Ford prototype, recently unearthed from its desert hiding place. Although the Army turned its nose up at the body design, it was still one of the two Ford pilot models. Owner Jeff Polidoro is planning a slow, careful restoration of the vehicle.

in debt, but by selling much of his personal real estate, obtaining an 18-month grace period from his creditors and embarking on an extended trip to convince dealers to keep the faith, the persuasive J. N. Willys was able turn the company completely around. By 1923, Willys had not only paid off his debts but showed a $13,000,000 profit.

Willys-Overland faced more challenges and had triumphs through the 1930s, but many of those were without J. N. Willys. He was appointed Ambassador to Poland in the late 1920s. By mid-1933, Willys-Overland was again in trouble and J. N. Willys was asked to come back and take the reins again for the sake of the Toledo, Ohio, city economy, which he did. A cerebral embolism on August 26, 1935, ended J. N. Willys' efforts to make another comeback.

In 1936, the company reorganized into Willys-Overland Motors under the financial leadership of Ward Canaday, but the late 1930s was not overly prosperous for the new W-O. It had little more than a small slice of the car market (a high of about 2 percent) and a tenuous niche building stylish, economical mid-sized cars.

Like Bantam, Willys had pursued government contracts. In December 1938, W-O had offered the Army a chance to test drive one of its small cars. The first response was a friendly "no thanks," but through gentle coercion, the government was convinced to test the vehicle in January 1939 at Fort Knox, Kentucky. The results were predictable, given the limited performance of a standard sedan off the highway: another "not interested, thanks."

A more direct connection to the Jeep story came in March of 1940, when W-O president Charles Frazer and chief engineer Barney Roos were

asked to observe the Howie-Wiley Bellyflopper in action and make comments. Roos was able to put together some suggestions that no doubt began the creative engineering juices flowing for the gifted engineer. When the opportunity to bid came a few months later, Willys was forewarned, but the bureaucracy within the organization still moved slowly. When the July 22 bid deadline rolled around, the company had produced little more than rough sketches and some very preliminary specifications.

Ford Motor Company

The bedrock for the Ford Motor Company was, is, and always will be the dynamic Henry Ford. Ford built his first gas engine in 1887, his first car in 1896, and formed the Ford Motor Company in 1903. He was a gifted self-taught engineer, a ruthless competitor, and a benevolent boss. Ford perfected the assembly-line building techniques that became an auto industry standard and became famous for building simple, durable cars at a price most Americans could afford.

The exploits of Henry Ford and his company prior to 1940 have filled volumes, so there is little need to rehash them here. Unlike the other two "founding fathers" of the jeep, Ford Motor Company was a large, healthy, productive, well-founded company at the time the specifications for the proposed quarter-ton were released. No late night scrambles or the quiet desperation of a company hanging on the edge happened at Ford. FoMoCo was a profitable, successful company doing a good job for its stockholders. This fact has made the FoMoCo part of the jeep story much less dramatic, and therefore much less exciting for writers to delve into.

By 1940, Henry Ford was semi-retired and his son Edsel had control over military contracts. It's clear that Edsel Ford, who eventually was the major supporter of the quarter-ton idea, had little initial interest in the proposed contract. At the time, the Ford Motor Company (FoMoCo) was involved in competing for several other military contracts, to include the half-ton 4x4. To a degree, Ford had to be sweet-talked into taking an interest. Knowledgeable forces high on the military procurement food-chain knew that neither Bantam nor Willys were capable of high production numbers coming out of the gate. This was a legitimate concern, as was the dispersion of facilities in case of attack or sabotage. Ford had several plants capable of building jeeps. Bantam and Willys had one each.

FoMoCo was indeed courted and some serious angst was generated by Ford's behind-the-scene inclusion into the "jeep wars." Bantam and Willys also had their pundits and inside men. When it came to money or survival (in the case of Bantam and W-O), they all played virtually the same back-room games. The Ford people were just better at it. FoMoCo watched and planned as Bantam and Willys duked it out for the first contract.

The First Contract

The first contract was a daunting one. It specified a pilot model due in 49 days. That vehicle would be tested for 30 days and if it survived without a breakdown lasting more than 24 hours, the winner would be eligible for a contract for 70 more vehicles, 62 two-wheel steer and 8 four-wheel steer, to

THE FIRST QUARTER-TON
DESIGN SPECIFICATIONS

These are some of the specifications the military gave manufacturers to build a vehicle around. With these specifications, the manufacturers were faced with an almost impossible task. Add to that the daunting task of producing a pilot model in only 49 days, and then producing another 69 vehicles in just 75 days. It's no wonder only two manufacturers of the 135 contacted replied. The specifications were subsequently revised several times to a more practical level as the realities of physics asserted themselves during tests of the pilot models.

	Original Requirements	Amended Requirements		Original Requirements	Amended Requirements
Air Filter	oil bath type		Engine	none specified	four-cylinder specified with no aluminum head
Armament	.30 cal MG on pedestal mount		Maximum height	36 inches	40 inches
Axles	full-floating		Maximum speed	50mph on-road	
Approach Angle	45 degrees		Personnel Capacity	3 persons	
Body	Rectangular w/folding windshield		Towing	provision for	braced pintle hitch specified
Departure Angle	40 degrees		Weight	1,200 pounds	1,275 pounds
Drivetrain	four-wheel drive, w/2-speed transfer case		Wheelbase	75 inches	80 inches

be built in another 75 days. Two bids were received, one each from Bantam and Willys. Ford lurked nearby, thinking the 49-day schedule was impossible. When the envelopes were opened, the Willys bid was nominally lower than Bantam's, but Willys would not commit to the 49-day pilot model time frame and its tentative design specs did not meet the Army requirements as closely as Bantam's. Bantam's bid was accepted on July 25, 1940, with the official acceptance date listed as 5 August.

Just about everyone in the industry was betting against Bantam. Karl Probst later reported the betting as 5:1 against. In Probst's initial planning, it was determined that little of Bantam's major automobile hardware was suitable for use in the new quarter-ton. Most pieces had to be sourced from outside vendors. The engine came from Continental Motors, the transmission from Warner Gear, the transfer case and axles from Spicer. A hundred smaller, but no less important parts came from other suppliers. A major part of the undertaking was ramrodding the suppliers into producing on time. Bantam's future was on the line if even a few of the parts did not arrive in time.

Besides Probst, three other men were vital to the assembly of the pilot model. Harold Crist was the plant manager. He had a long history with cars going back to the early days of Duesenberg and a stint as a race car driver. He had a reputation for being able to take a pile of metal shavings and make almost anything. In many ways, Crist's dedication and ability to make

something from nothing was largely responsible for the successful completion of the pilot model in the 49-day period. Probst called him a human dynamo. Chester Hemphling and Ralph Turner were also pivotal in getting the hand-built Bantam pilot together in time.

It all came together on September 21, when the Bantam pilot model was given its first spin around the block. Crist had the honor of being the first man to drive a jeep. This trial run included a climb up a 40-degree hill. A quick cross country test showed Bantam what the company already suspected, this vehicle was the best off-road vehicle in the world at that moment in time. After about 150 miles of shakedowns and tuning, the Bantam Reconnaissance Car, soon to be known as "Old Number One," was given the green light for delivery.

On September 23, the contract due date, Probst and Crist left Butler for the 230-mile drive to Camp Holabird, Maryland. They arrived that afternoon, just 30 minutes prior to the 5 P.M. deadline. A number of Holabird staff were on hand to greet Probst and Crist and to view the new Bantam. Among those present was Maj. Herbert Lawes, the Purchasing and Contract Officer. After observing the Bantam tackling some obstacles, he personally took the little 4x4 on a brutal 15-minute test drive. Afterwards, this officer who had driven every vehicle the Army had tested or owned in 20 years is reported to have said, "I believe this unit will make history."

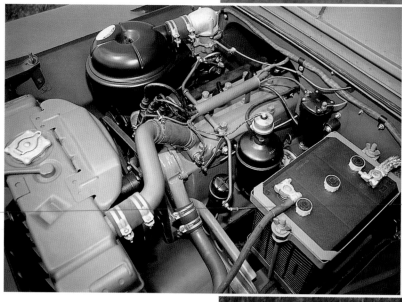

The Ford GP made its debut soon enough to be used by the American Volunteer Group (AVG), a.k.a the Flying Tigers, in China during much of 1942. This restored GP jeep is painted up as an AVG vehicle and is quite snazzy with its roundels. Almost 4,500 GPs were built and they are the most common remaining pre-standardized type. The Flying Tigers destroyed 286 enemy planes with only eight losses.

Old Number One

From September 27 to October 16, 1940, the Bantam pilot was put through a torture test specifically designed to rip the vehicle apart. Captain Eugene Mosley, chief of testing, led the small group of vehicular sadism specialists who had a reputation for being able to break anything. The Bantam was no exception. After 3,400 miles, only 247 on highways, the test was terminated when the Bantam's chassis broke in two places. Nobody was surprised, since Mosley had been seen jumping the vehicle off a four-foot-high loading dock. The chassis was repaired overnight, but Mosley had seen enough to give the Bantam a thumbs-up.

The final test report yielded 20 faults of various kinds. Some were outside parts that failed, including an exploded generator pulley. Others were design issues, such as not being able to fit chains on the rear tires due to inadequate fender clearance. For a first effort, however, the Army regarded the vehicle as a success and said so in its typically laconic way, "The vehicle demonstrated ample power and all requirements of the service."

Old Number One disappeared some time in early 1941 after being involved in a collision with a utility truck. Factory workers remember it being torn down for repairs but its ultimate fate is unknown. One legend has it being stripped of useful mechanical pieces and buried on the grounds as scrap. My opinion is that it was likely recycled into a BRC 60, which was a similar vehicle. "Waste not, want not" was a way of life in an auto company hanging on the edge of financial ruin.

Bantam BRC 60

After the successful test of the pilot model, Bantam was granted a contract to build 70 more vehicles of an updated design. At the same time Old Number One was being tested, Bantam was gearing up to build the new version. The Bantam Reconnaissance Car, Model 60, or BRC 60 for short (also known as the Mark II), was similar in construction to the pilot model. Obvious

visible differences were the more military-looking angular fenders and the enlarged door openings.

The BRC 60s were given to actual Army units to test in day-to-day use. It was as much an opportunity to see how they could be used as it was a physical test of the vehicle. The Army had yet to discover the full range of versatility offered by the quarter-ton design. In fact, the Army was never able to test the full limits of the quarter-ton's versatility.

The Army units who tested the BRCs were enthusiastic. They were found to be useful in every arm of the service. The little 4x4s were frequently seen in Army maneuvers that were becoming more common as war loomed ahead. In a little more than a few months, the BRC 60s were returned and replaced by updated quarter-tons. The BRC 60s were among the first jeeps sold surplus, as early as 1943. The biggest dealer at that time, Berg's of Chicago, is known to be the first retailer of surplus jeeps and a yard photo of the place during that time shows one tired BRC 60. Only one BRC 60 is known to have survived and is owned by the Smithsonian.

The Willys Quad

On November 13, 1940, as Bantam produced the BRC 60, Willys rolled out their own champion in the jeep wars, the "Quad." Two versions were submitted: a two-wheel and a four-wheel steer. Even as it learned the original contract bid had failed, Willys was encouraged by government insiders to design and build a prototype at its own expense. Evidently, Willys execs considered it a good risk. Representatives from Willys had been on hand to view the Bantam pilot and learn from the tests. In theory, this should have given them an edge in making the vehicle an Army favorite, but it didn't.

Even though the Army had finally received a dose of reality and raised the weight limit to 2,160 pounds, Roos couldn't get the Quad down to "fighting" weight. The first completed Willys pilot model started out at 2,520 pounds, 360 pounds over the limit required for eligibility. That didn't stop the Army from accepting it for tests under a contract that put it under no obligations whatsoever, except to furnish a written evaluation.

The Quad did fine in the series of tests, but not as spectacularly as some historians have reported. While the extra power of the larger engine was evident, much of that power was used up in hauling around the extra bulk. There were two major engine failures reportedly due to inadequate air filters, a major transmission failure due to overheating, a transfer case failure, an unusual number of spring failures, and numerous problems with body items, such as the windshield brackets. The chassis also failed after 5,100 miles. The breakages and failures did not concern the Army. The tests were designed to uncover faults, and all of the faults were fixable in a later, improved model. What concerned the Army most was weight, and of Willys-Overland's apparent lack of willingness to do much about it.

Willys' bid of $959 per vehicle for a 1,500-vehicle contract had been accepted as the low one, although it was only $3.39 lower than Bantam's. Winning a contract was contingent upon the company producing a satisfactory pilot model. After reviewing the Holabird test report, the technical subcommittee ruled that Willys had not submitted a satisfactory pilot model due to weight considerations. Despite this, on January 7, 1941, the Adjutant General overruled the subcommittee's findings and approved the vehicle as "satisfactory," opening the door for Willys to produce 1,500 updated vehicles. So much howling ensued from Bantam, Ford, and their pundits that eventually, the Army decided to purchase 1,500 vehicles from each manufacturer.

There is a great story commonly told about Willys chief engineer Barney Roos stripping the Quad down to a pile of parts and having every piece examined for ways to reduce weight. That story is told out of context, and actually applies to the later MA model. There was virtually no hope of getting the Quad down far enough to meet Army requirements.

The fate of the test Quads is a big mystery. The four-wheel-steer Quad is hardly mentioned. With Willys ending up with the lion's share of the glory over the development of the jeep, these prototypes are a source of great interest to historians and collectors. One Quad was seen as late as 1952, when it was posed for a photo alongside an MB, an M-38, and the M-38A1.

The Ford Pygmy and Budd

When Ford Motor Company jumped on the jeep bandwagon, it almost knocked Bantam and Willys off. Between the lobby power it possessed and the fine prototype it built, FoMoCo had the tiger by the tail. The FoMoCo hierarchy didn't show much interest in the idea until early October 1940, when the company received an invitation to bid on a large quarter-ton contract. Certain elements in the sales department had been hard at work promoting the idea since the Bantam won the initial bid. Engineer Dale Roeder was given the project to ramrod, and on October 16, sent a draftsman to Holabird to make sketches of the Bantam pilot. Roeder could be regarded as Ford's version of Harold Crist or Barney Roos. Clarence Kramer did most of the

design work on the GP and could be regarded as the equivalent of Probst, each the fathers of their particular jeep variant.

By late October, Roeder and staff had a working design and sent off numerous blueprints for manufacture of parts. Two identical chassis were built. One remained at Ford to have a body designed and built and the other went to Budd, a noted coachbuilder, for the same treatment. Roeder reported that both vehicles were complete by Thanksgiving Day 1940 and were shipped to Holabird for evaluation.

It was apparent right away that the Army did not like the Budd-bodied unit's general layout. In many ways, including visually, it was a near clone of the Model 60 Bantam. It appreciated the Kramer designed unit's control layout, low silhouette, and flat hood (useful for map reading, eating, and other things). The Ford's general layout, with a few variations, was eventually adopted as the standard for the quarter-tons. Many other small details from the GP found their way into the standardized model nearly a year later.

The Ford was powered by a variant of the Ford N tractor engine, which itself was a half of a 1939 Mercury V8. The two pilot models used the same low-mounted updraft carb as the tractor. This became a problem the first time the unit was tested in water and the fuel system was quickly changed to a downdraft Holley. Much has been made of the Ford engine's lack of power. The engine was a virtual equal of the Bantam in the power department, but given the Bantam's slight weight advantage, the Ford was a little slower. Period documents indicate that Ford was prepared to increase the displacement of this engine should the need arise. Common lore also has the Ford engine as not reliable. With the exception of a cranky carburetor and a funky coil, little documentation exists to support that claim.

Like the W-O pilot model, the Ford pilot was also overweight, in this case by some 130 pounds. This fact had not escaped Ford engineers. By November 28, 1940, just five days after the pilot models had been delivered, a memo from the sales department notified all concerned parties of the engineering improvements already worked out that would reduce the weight deficit to a mere 29 pounds on an improved model. These pounds were eventually eliminated as well.

One of the controversial aspects to the Ford entry has been that the weight limit was raised from 2,075 pounds to 2,160 pounds, or 2,175 pounds with a machine gun mount in place. The weight limit was, in fact, raised partly as a bit of reality by the government and partly as a compromise for Ford lowering the cowl height to 2 inches below the 40-inch specification.

Somewhere along the line, the Ford pilot acquired the nickname "Pygmy." It isn't known when this name was applied, but the name appeared in a large number of magazine articles. Ford Jeep expert Jim Gilmore's extensive research shows that "Blitz Buggy" was the favored term with the Ford crowd. The original Ford Pygmy has survived, as has the original Budd-bodied Ford.

The Bantam BRC 40

After a great deal of turmoil, Bantam was issued a contract for 1,500 improved vehicles. The result was the BRC 40 (Bantam Reconnaissance Car, Model 40). The BRC 40 was Bantam's closest brush with volume jeep pro-

duction. Subsequent orders led to a total of 2,605 units, 1,175 Series Is and 1,430 Series IIs. Bantam's last unit was produced in early December 1941, and the company never built another BRC 40 except to assemble a few yard hacks or prototypes. It scrambled and found useful and profitable work building torpedoes for the British, aircraft landing gear, and the famous quarter-ton Bantam jeep trailer. Bantam did not survive long after World War II. The company was sold to ARMCO Steel in the mid-1950s.

The last Bantams embodied all that the company had learned but because these were still pre-standardized jeeps, they still carried the individual earmarks of the Bantam Company. Light, nimble, and fuel-efficient cars were Bantam trademarks and the last BRCs embodied them all.

It's been noted that the three pre-standardized designs were all similar in execution. In some ways, the Bantam was the most unique of the three. The chassis is an example. Rather than using the more common C-channel design, Bantam used an inverted U-section chassis that was plated on the bottom for extra strength. The body of the early models also had corrugated sheet metal under the floor for reinforcement.

While the drivetrain was similar in all three rigs, Bantam used a Warner Gear T-84 trans, but with a lower input torque rating than the T-84 used in the MA. The BRC and GP shared the feature of Spicer axles with differentials offset to the left side. The BRC's axles were called Model 40s. The Model 18 Spicer transfer case outputs matched the axle offsets.

The engine used for the Bantam was a commercial grade Continental Motors BY-4112 that displaced 112 cubic inches. It was adapted from a forklift application and had been used in stationary applications and other industrial purposes. A slightly larger model 4124 (124-ci) engine was available at the same time, but it isn't clear why it wasn't chosen. Not long after the jeep story was all said and done, Continental enlarged that basic design to a 58-horsepower, 160-ci variant that was only marginally heavier than the smaller unit.

The Ford GP

The GP was a well-built pre-standardized jeep that has been highly underrated and much maligned since 1941. In many ways, the GP was the general pattern from which the standardized World War II jeep was sculpted. The grille, flat hood, forward-folding windshield design, rear seat, and control layout were all largely derived from the GP. Small but well-known details such as the spring-loaded "T" handle hood holddowns also came from the GP.

The GP was an upgrade from the pilot model. The GP was largely the same, but considerably lighter. It was built in the largest numbers of all the pre-standardized units, with 4,458 units built from February to November 1941, with a couple showing up on January 1942 production sheets. The GP was also exported in the largest numbers and ended up in the hands of Allied forces all over the world.

The GP was much like its Bantam or Willys counterparts and used axles built either by Spicer or by Ford to Spicer designs. When Spicer got way behind producing axles, Ford lent it the tooling to keep it ahead of demand. At one point, the delayed return of these tools briefly stopped GP production altogether.

The Willys MA is a rare find, even when it was built in 1941. Only 1,555 were produced from June to September 1941, and since the standardized unit came out November of that year, they had a relatively short time for field testing. Similar to the other pre-standardized quarter-tons, after being replaced by the standardized jeeps with front-line units, they were gradually phased out of military service. Many ended up working in civilian government service livery. A large batch of MAs were sent to Eastern Europe after the war to aid in recovery there. This is another Ken Hake restoration. There are only 27 MAs known to still exist. When a correctly restored example comes up for sale, the price is usually near $60,000.

The transmission was an adaptation of a Ford three-speed once used in the Model A Ford. It was known for being reliable, but was clunky in operation. It was mated to a Spicer Model 18 transfer case that was similar to what the Bantam used.

The GP engine was an adaptation of the 9N tractor engine that was developed for the Fordson tractor the previous year. The camshaft was altered in the GP version to supply a more flexible rpm range, and later the updraft carb, used briefly in the Pygmy, was later updated to a downdraft Holley. If the GP engine had one notorious problem, it was this Holley one-barrel. The problem still exists today. The carb was so poor that when the GPs were sold surplus, irate owners often junked the unit in favor of whatever could be bolted up. As a result, surviving GPs with original carbs are very rare today. Few other changes were made from the engine's initial use in the Pygmy.

The term "GP" is also the source of incorrect information. It's sometimes said the slurring of GP to "GEEEP" is the source of the jeep name and that GP is for "General Purpose." The former gets refuted later in this book, but the 1941 Ford parts numbering system lists "G" as a government contract vehicle and "P" as the 80-inch-wheelbase reconnaissance car.

The Willys MA

The MA was W-O's preproduction model that was built under the three-way contracts for 1,500 units from each manufacturer. It was the last pre-standardized jeep to appear, and only 1,555 units were built from June to

September 1941. As a result of its late arrival, the MA received only a fraction of the field testing that the Ford or Bantam jeeps underwent. Unlike Bantam or Ford, there were no major supplemental orders for MAs. That was partly to do with Willys running behind on production and the fact it was awarded a contract for 16,000 standardized jeeps in July 1941.

Mechanically, the MA was a virtual clone of the Quad. It's a small wonder given that performance was not an issue. It did receive an improved air cleaner, a weakness that had killed two Quad engines. The body was clearly influenced by the Ford and Bantam pilots, but it retained a front-end look that was uniquely Willys.

The MA was a sprightly performer. It was the lightest Willys jeep ever built and combined with the 60-horsepower engine, it could move out with relative authority. During its design process, low weight was still one of the primary government edicts. Roos managed to get the unit down to the prescribed 2,160 pounds but warned that too much strength had been taken out in the process. He was proven right. The MA's thin sheet metal was notorious for cracking, and the rear-mounted spare tire was known for tearing out of the panel. Roos had traded body weight for engine weight. The Go-Devil engine was some 65 pounds heavier than the Bantam's Continental engine.

And the Winner Is . . .

What must be remembered is that the testing given to all three vehicles was to determine whether they were "satisfactory" for military service. All three were deemed satisfactory. After that, it was simply a matter of who submitted the lowest bid. When the time came for the first big contract for 16,000 standardized quarter-tons, Willys won the bid. It's as simple as that.

It must also be remembered that Willys did benefit from a controversial decision with regard to the vastly overweight Quad being a "satisfactory" pilot or not. If the Quartermaster General had not lobbied on behalf of buying pre-standardized quarter-tons from all three of the manufacturers (most likely *not* a position taken to benefit W-O), we might have had a different ending to this story.

History has shown that in terms of overall benefit, W-O reaped the largest corporate gains from the development of the jeep in World War II. Not detracting from W-O's product, it must be recognized that this fact had as much to do with W-O's great advertising department as anything. The company wasted no effort to market the wartime jeep as a Willys baby.

The question remains: Which of the three pre-standardized jeeps was really the best? This is a difficult question to answer 60 years later, but let's let the Army speak.

A number of field tests were done between March and September 1941 with Army units. The units received the pre-standardized vehicles, used them as needed and filed reports on each vehicle. The Willys MA didn't participate in many of the tests because it didn't arrive until mid- to late July. Therefore, most of the test data was compiled on the Ford and Bantam, the more promptly delivered vehicles. The Fords began arriving in large numbers by mid-March, and the Bantams arrived by mid- to late April. Fords were the most common jeep by far. The initial Ford and Bantam contracts were completed long before Willys had delivered its first MA. The test data was used largely to pick out the best features or show the need for changes rather than to determine which was the "best" vehicle.

Just before issuing a contract for 16,000 standardized jeeps, someone in the government finally thought to test the three pre-standardized models directly against each other. These tests were done at Fort Benning, Georgia, by the Infantry starting in June 1941. They were somewhat delayed while awaiting the delivery of an MA, which finally arrived June 26. The MA, BRC-40, and GP were run against each other in a series of performance and design feature tests that simulated a real world military situation.

When the smoke cleared, the Willys won in many of the performance areas, including acceleration, top speed, grade ability, and cross country travel. This was directly related to the power and torque edge of the Go-Devil engine. In rough ground hill-climbing tests, the MA could crawl up a grade with reserves of torque, while the Bantam struggled and the Ford was often stopped. Out on the highway, the Willys could crank out a 74-mile-per-hour top speed, versus 64 for the Bantam and 59 for the Ford. The Willys had the lowest fuel economy (20.2 miles per gallon).

With regards to technical issues, the Willys was rated as having the best transmission, best radiator, and strongest chassis. The Willys was downgraded in several technical areas, including the carburetor, column shift, parking brake, and springs.

Because of its light weight, the Bantam shone in the fuel mileage department (23.2 miles per gallon) as well as in braking performance. Testers also liked its precise steering and nimble feel. Technically, the Bantam was downgraded for carburetor problems and vulnerable front brake lines.

The Ford did not take any "bests" in the performance area, although the testers found it adequate in all performance areas. Technically, the Ford was downgraded for a poor shifting transmission (gear-grinding and an imprecise shifter), carb flooding on angles, and imprecise steering.

In areas secondary to performance (today's term being ergonomics), the Ford was the clear winner. Testers liked the interior arrangement, driver comfort, and overall body layout. They especially liked the front-end arrangement, low silhouette, and flat hood. The GP and Bantam tops were both downgraded for being difficult to erect. The MA was downgraded for driver comfort, although the testers at Holabird seemed to like it. The MA was given credit for the best top.

So which was best? The Army said, "The standard vehicle should be based on the Willys chassis with the Ford shifter and handbrake arrangement, and performance characteristics of the Willys." Willys went on to make the low bid and build the standardized units under the new 16,000-unit contract. The standardized units homogenized the best features of all three pre-standardized vehicles into one. The only truly unique Willys feature in the standardized units was the engine. This turned out to be a good thing. As operational necessities and standardized components brought the weight back up (to near Quad weight as it turns out), the larger engine helped maintain a reasonably good power-to-weight ratio.

REFINEMENTS AND TRIUMPHS IN WORLD WAR II

Prior to December 7, 1941, the only war in the jeep world was the one that had raged between the three companies clamoring for jeep contracts. Willys-Overland was just beginning to turn out standardized model MB units. Production had started on November 18, and a good deal of Spicer's output was going to Willys to build jeeps. There were occasional slowdowns and stoppages due to lack of axles or transfer cases.

In October 1941, Ford's vast production capacity was tapped to produce standardized jeeps. After gauging the potential profit or loss and judging the importance to the war effort, it had grudgingly agreed to produce a government standardized quarter-ton, even though the retooling expenses were astronomical. A shortage of machine tools to produce items such as axles, transfer cases, constant velocity joints, and universal joints left it up to Ford to guarantee production of these items to get the contract. In the end, Ford produced most of it in-house.

The Ford GP evolved into the GPW in early 1942. Although Ford originated the slat-type grille in the GP model and this basic design was adopted for the standardized model, documentation exists that indicate Ford developed the more familiar stamped grille as a labor-saving device, received permission from the government to substitute the grille, and included it in its GPW when production started in January 1942.

By the time of the attack on Pearl Harbor, Bantam was largely out of the picture, having just delivered its last BRC-40 the day before the bombing. Despite six months of future protests and putting a U.S. Senator on the case, Bantam could never convince the government of the company's ability to produce significant numbers of standardized quarter-tons without a major strain on the already-backlogged machine tool industry. Yes, the builder of the first jeep got a raw deal, but it was less about greedy corporations than it was about circumstance, emergency war planning, and sheer bad luck.

Blooded: Jeeps at War

No Jeep history is complete without a war story or two. When combat units began receiving the latest jeeps, they went to work finding ways to exceed the design limits. As Willys and Ford churned out jeeps to the tune of 640,000 vehicles by the end of the war, they became as familiar to the GI as his rifle.

The earliest and most spectacular use of jeeps in combat was in 1941–1942 by the British in North Africa. Equipping the vehicles with up to four heavy machine guns and loaded beyond capacity with ammo and fuel, the British Long Range Desert Group detachment of the elite SAS (Special Air Service) made jeep raids far behind enemy lines, destroying vital supplies. In one raid, a line of jeeps crisscrossed a German airfield far behind enemy lines, machine guns blazing, and destroyed every aircraft without a single loss. The Germans were impressed enough with the jeep to issue a general order that captured jeeps should be used wherever possible to replace their own inadequate machines.

Later on, in the Pacific Theater, a jeep was credited with destroying four Japanese tanks. With a 37mm anti-tank gun strapped to the jeep's hood, two Marines darted in and out of the tanks firing at point-blank range. Early jeeps were used in the Philippines to pull rail cars of ammunition to the front after the locomotives were destroyed. Equipped with flanged wheels, the jeeps pulled 20-ton rail cars around the clock to keep the troops supplied with ammo. One battered jeep was officially issued a Purple Heart medal after being damaged in two successive Pacific beach landings and was sent home; the mechanical equivalent of what the GIs called a "million dollar" wound.

In North Africa, Italy, and mainland Europe, jeeps not only endured extremes of temperatures, abuse and neglect, they suffered from the ravages of bullets, artillery, and bombs. Battle-ravaged jeeps littered the countryside after the fighting stopped. They were collected and shipped back to rear echelon depots to be rebuilt and sent back to the battlefield. It was said that the working life of a jeep on the front lines was a month.

The jeep also offered the GI an outlet for his youthful exuberance in the form of a sports car. Sports car? The jeep had a better power-to-weight ratio than many of the contemporary automobiles. Light and low slung, it actually cornered well for the day. Unfortunately, since the jeep lacked a roll cage or roof, rollovers were usually fatal, as many GIs found out. Bill Mauldin, the famous World War II cartoonist, said, "Jeeps killed about as many people as any weapon in World War II. You have to drive it with respect."

At the beginning of World War II, the Kfz. 1 *Kübelwagen* ("Bucket Car") was the jeep's major competition. It was no contest. The German rig has a 985cc, 24-horsepower engine and was a 4x2. The chassis was based on the Volkswagen. It had the weight advantage, but was no match when the going got tough. A captured *Kübel* is shown here while under tests at the Aberdeen Proving Grounds alongside a Slat-Grille MB. The German Army had standing orders to capture and use jeeps at every opportunity.

Right

Production of the standardized quarter-ton began in November 1940 by Willys. The first 25,808 were called Slat-Grilles, for their welded strip-steel grilles. Besides the grille, most early MBs were distinctive in their square fuel tank tub and embossed "Willys" emblem on the rear panel. Very early Slat-Grilles had the low MA windshield, and only the last 5,100 used a glove box.

By the end of the war, there was scarcely one GI who didn't have an abiding love for the jeep, and many hungered to have one at home. With all the souvenirs and "liberated" material being sent home in footlockers and duffel bags, it wouldn't be surprising to find that some enterprising GI found a way to build a "Johnny Cash" jeep by sending one home in pieces. Surplus jeeps were sold in Europe to GIs who used them during the Army of Occupation, and some brought them home.

In occupied Germany and war-torn Europe, a huge problem existed with stolen jeeps. You could step away for five minutes and find your jeep gone. The trusty jeep did not have an ignition key to keep men honest; it just had an on-off switch. Elaborate anti-theft devices were developed by the Army, the most common being a large chain wrapped around the steering wheel and pedals. Even then, jeep thefts were common.

Early Standardized: Willys MB Slat-Grille

The standardized quarter-ton put all the best ideas into one package. By operational necessity, the Willys MB had gained back all the weight Barney

The jeep is probably a write-off, but the GI will live to fight again. The incident was an accident on a muddy road and not combat related. This shot was taken by the author's father in Germany during the spring of 1945. R.P.Allen

General Omar Bradley inspects a GPW destined for the commander of the 1st Ukrainian Army as a gift from the U.S. 12th Army. National Archives

Left
A Willys MB bypasses a minefield on a muddy track near Pratella, Italy, on November 1, 1943. The extremely wet winter of that year tested the limits of military transport. It was one of the worst winters of the war and the GIs not only had to fight the enemy, but floods and mud. *U.S. Army*

Roos had worked so hard to remove. It hovered at around 2,450 pounds, and Roos' choice to hang in there with the heavy Go-Devil engine was fully justified.

Later nicknamed "Slat-Grilles" for their welded steel grilles, the early MBs were a work in progress. The production records show 25,808 Slat-Grilles were produced from November 18, 1941, to March 6, 1942. There were many design changes in the Slat-Grille during that time. Just a few of the first 3,545 were built using the short MA-style windshield. The early units used a squared-off fuel tank tub, while the later ones used the more familiar rounded tub. The last 5,112 Slat-Grilles came with glove boxes. Slat-Grilles wore an embossed "Willys" logo on the left side of the rear panel.

Early Standardized: Ford GPW Script

The first Ford jeeps made their debut on January 6, 1942, and continued with production until July 30, 1945. The term "GPW" is the Ford Engineering term that breaks down to: G = Government contract vehicle, P = 80-inch-wheelbase reconnaissance car, and W = Willys engine.

The first Fords were considerably different from the early Willys or the later Ford or Willys, although the parts largely interchanged as per specification. The "Script" in the section heading signifies the first 17,000 units that wore an embossed Ford logo on the rear panel. This was discontinued at the

AN ENDURING MYTH:
THE JEEP-IN-A-CRATE

The enduring myth of jeeps-in-a-crate has spread like a weed through the jeep world from after World War II through today. There is always somebody's "Uncle Joe" who knows someone who knew someone who bought a jeep-in-a-crate for $50, or knew of a bunch of jeeps buried in a desert somewhere. While some jeeps were shipped overseas in crates, they were rapidly reassembled at depots when they arrived. Noted author and jeep historian Ray Cowdery has a standing $50,000 offer for a legitimate jeep-in-a-crate and nobody has come forth in over 15 years. Trust him and me: the only legitimate remaining jeeps-in-a-crate are the ones that have been rotting in the holds of sunken cargo ships for over 50 years.

The mythical jeep-in-a-crate recreated. The Georgia Chapter of the MVPA studied manuals and hundreds of photos and reproduced this crated GPW. This is how many jeeps arrived in Europe. This display was the hit of the 1997 MVPA Convention at Memphis.

at the Army's insistence on both Ford and Willys models. There would be no advertising at the government's expense!

The first few thousand GPWs used what has become known as "transitional chassis." While Ford's chassis maker, the Murray Corp., was tooling up to build its own version of the standardized chassis, it bought Willys-spec units from the Midland Steel Company. They were missing the Willys serial number tag, but had the mounting plate for it. This has confused and confounded GPW restorers for decades! After that, the Ford line was geared up and the chassis became uniquely Ford, although it freely interchanged with the Willys. See the *Viva La Difference* sidebar for more Willys/Ford differences.

One of the major differences between early Willys and Fords is the grille. The stamped sheet-metal grille appeared on the Ford from day one, while Willys did not adopt it until April 1942. Noted historian Jim Gilmore has interviewed early Ford engineers and uncovered documents that would indicate it was designed by Clarence Kramer, a Ford engineer. Apparently, this was done as a labor-saving device because the welded grille specified in the contract was time consuming to make. Ironic, isn't it? One of the most unique automotive features of all time began as a labor saving device.

In Gilmore's interview with Kramer in 1993, Kramer said, "Ford Motor Company needed approval on the use of the one piece stamping replace-

ment from the strip steel design brush guard that was approved as part of the prototype vehicle approved by the Army. This is a normal requirement on all government contracts of this type." This all becomes very interesting because the design of the jeep grille is a trademarked item held by Daimler Chrysler. Incidentally, Kramer was probably the most responsible for the "nuts-and-bolts" design work on the GP and the GPW.

Late Standardized: Willys MB

From the adoption of the stamped grille in early 1942, the MB remained largely the same until January 1944. At that time, Ford was building bodies in-house, and Willys was having American Central Manufacturing build its units. While interchangeable, there were significant differences in minor details. In order to facilitate interchangeability, Ford and Willys agreed to have American Central build a composite body that included features of both bodies. Both companies used these composite bodies until the end of production. MB production ended on September 21, 1945, with a total of 361,339 units.

Late Standardized: Ford GPW

Until January 1944, the Ford remained largely as shown in the *Viva La Difference* sidebar. After that time, the composite body appeared to further homogenize the standardized jeeps. Detail differences remained and one of

Easy duty! The "Seep" was the amphibious version of the jeep that was built by Ford. Almost 13,000 units were produced. These GIs are obviously enjoying their training cruise. *U.S. Army*

The GPA had a slightly longer wheelbase than the standard GPW (84 inches versus 80) and was about 1,000 pounds heavier. The ribbing on the hull is for strength. The hull was made of fairly light gauge sheet metal. *U.S. Army*

them was that Ford marked virtually every part, from nuts and bolt up, with a script "F." According to popular legend, this edict came from Henry Ford himself, who did not want to deal with warranty claims on Willys parts.

Water Jeeps: Ford GPA "Seep"

Back in 1940, when the tentative specs for the jeep were being laid out, the Army expressed a desire for an amphibious variant. The idea didn't get serious consideration until after the standard quarter-ton 4x4 was well under way. In April 1941, the National Defense Research Committee set out to work out the details of a whole line of military amphibs under a program designated QMC-4. Out of this study group, the 2-1/2 ton DUKW "Duck" idea emerged, as well as specs for the quarter-ton amphibious vehicle.

In order to facilitate development, the naval architects at Sparkman & Stephens were asked in July 1941 to design a mechanism for a floating jeep. The idea evolved into a watertight hull that carried the basic quarter-ton running gear, and the firm developed a scowlike design.

Some jeeps were modified by the branch of service where it was employed. In this case, the USMC-modified quarter-tons were designed to carry two litters and two medics. The medical storage box, rear door, and brackets were fabricated. These units were quite successful in the Pacific Theater, where larger ambulances were hampered by jungles and tight quarters. This restored unit is the only known remaining example.

The MB-T "Super Jeep" was a 6x6 version of the wartime jeep that was intended to bolster a shortage of 3/4 ton trucks. It was a successful but redundant design. Shown here is the Air Corps version, which had the largest quantity built (a total of 16 for tests). Commonly known as the "Tug," it was often tested with a fifth wheel, and in this case, a Fruehauf trailer specifically built for the vehicles.

When the bullets quit flying, the Army of Occupation in Europe settled down to a fragile peace. The comfort, or lack thereof, of the wartime jeep became an issue on a continent where cold temperatures and rain were common. A number of hardtop and heater kits were developed for the quarter-ton. These rather stylish kits were made by Steyr in Austria. *R. P. Allen*

Marmon-Herrington was initially given the project and began work in October 1941. It was given three Willys MAs to provide the jeep components and as Sparkman & Stephens provided blueprints and patterns, M-H built a hull out of heavy gauge sheet metal. The unit did not use a separate chassis, and as a result, the QMC-4, as it became known, weighed a hefty 3,465 pounds.

Unfortunately for M-H, in December 1941, Ford also received the go-ahead to develop an amphibious vehicle. Ford's progress soon outpaced M-H's. Ford delivered a pilot model on February 2, 1942, and it took M-H until mid-March to provide the QMC-4. The first Ford prototype was based on the GPW model. Ford submitted two more prototypes in late March and mid-April for tests. In every area of testing, Ford's variant outperformed the M-H.

Although Ford was given a verbal go-ahead to begin production on April 11, GPA (G = Government contract, P = 80-inch-wheelbase reconnaissance car, A = Amphibian) production did not actually start until September. By April 26, 1943, more than 12,000 vehicles had been produced, and the last few units rolled off the Ford line on May 10, for a total of 12,778 vehicles.

The GPA used standard GPW mechanicals and had a similar but redesigned chassis that stretched the wheelbase to 84 inches. At 3,400 pounds, it was some 1,000 pounds heavier than a standard GPW. A PTO drove the three-bladed prop as well as a belt-driven bilge pump. A hand pump was also provided. An engine-driven capstan winch with a 3,500-pound capacity was fitted on the bow. All GPAs used 12-volt electrical systems.

The GPA was never regarded as completely successful. A U.S. Army Material Command pamphlet describes them as a "technical and tactical failure." Many of them sank in rough weather. Both the Russians and the Americans used amphibious vehicles in major campaigns and GPAs were most successful when crossing large rivers. They were not very successful in the Normandy beach landings of June 1944.

Experimental

Standardized jeeps provided the basis for countless experiments and specialized adaptations. One of the first was the Smart armored jeep. In collaboration with Willys, the Smart Engineering Company experimented with an armor kit in 1941. The first version was tested in November 1941 on a Willys MA and was given the experimental designation T-25. Later MA-based versions with altered characteristics were built and called the T-25E1, T-25E2, and T-25E3. Eventually, an armored kit was developed but it was seldom seen in service.

Another adaptation was the MB-L, a Willys attempt to compete in the flurry of extra light experimentation that went on in 1943. Willys engineers took an MB and stripped off every unnecessary item, and even a few semi-necessary ones, in order to make a 1,465-pound jeep suitable for air transport. Several pilot models were built, with the lightest using a body made mostly of plywood.

Interestingly, a project to build a plywood body for the standard jeep was also experimented with as a steel-saving measure. The Canadian-American

Truck Company built several types of wood bodies. The first was built out of solid oak and it outweighed the steel body. Plywood was experimented with, and proved largely successful, but plywood was just as high on the priority war materials list as steel.

In the early days of the jeep, a flanged-wheel conversion was built to allow jeeps to run on railroad tracks. According to many reports, this occurred in 1942 when jeeps were modified to tow ammunition trains in the battles to hold the Philippine Islands. In Europe, where rails were common, this conversion proved especially useful as rail yard switch engines and to haul supplies in captured railway rolling stock.

One of the more famous and fascinating experimental Jeeps of World War II was the "Super Jeeps": Willys Model MB-T. These were 3/4- or 1-ton

The early Ford GPW models are known as "Script" models because they have an embossed "Ford" in script on the rear panel. The blue identification numbers were used prior to 1943, when the army switched to white. Unlike MB engines that were painted Olive Drab (OD), Ford engines were gray. Ford engine and chassis numbers were the same, but the MB used different chassis and engine numbers.

USA 20420920

Avid Italian military vehicle collector Maurizio Beretta's 1943 MB is a genuine combat veteran. It is painted in Canadian markings to commemorate a certain event, although it was originally a U.S. Army jeep. After helping liberate Italy, the vehicle was left to the Italian Army. Note the overflow tank on the grille, which indicates the addition of a hot weather kit. *Maurizio Beretta*

FORD GPW vs. WILLYS MD:
VIVA LA DIFFERENCE!

Prior to the adoption of the composite body in January 1944, a plethora of differences existed between the Ford- and Willys-built standardized quarter-tons. Here are some of the more noteworthy differences. Some variations, most notably involving the chassis, remained after the composite body was changed.

The most readily visible difference between the GPW and MB is the front crossmember. The GPW has a C-channel piece, while the MB uses a tubular member.

The GPW serial number is stamped on the top of the chassis, between the front crossmember and the motor mount bracket on the driver's side. Occasionally, the serial number is found on the top rail between the bumper gusset and the radiator support bracket. The Willys number is on a tag riveted to a plate welded to the inside of the frame horn just behind the bumper area on the driver's side.

The transfer case shifter makes a rapid change in diameter at the top for the knob, and is also marked with a script "F" on the GPW. The MB shifter has a gradual taper.

The GPW rear crossmember has a small hole to the right of the bumperette, where the MB does not.

The engine hand crank and jack handles are marked with Ford script instead of with a W.O. (for Willys-Overland) on the GPW. Same goes for the jack handle.

The GPW toe board gussets have two smaller round holes and one large oval hole, while the Willys has five round holes of varying sizes. The body number for both vehicles can also be found on the underside of the toe board.

The GPW uses bolt clips on the springs while the MB uses clamps.

The ground strap from the generator to the regulator is separate on a GPW, but is wrapped up in a harness with the armature and field wires on an MB.

The reinforcing flange on the hinge end of the hood has no drain hole where the MB does have a drain hole. The general construction of the piece is distinctly different for each, although the hoods are interchangeable.

The rear shock brackets on a GPW are two stamped pieces welded together. The MB uses an open channel.

The rear seat supports on a GPW are roughly triangular in shape. The MB supports are roughly U-shaped.

The front frame horns on the GPW have a larger hole at the leading edge than does the MB.

The radiators on a GPW have fewer depressions on the top tank than the MB, and the MB depressions run continuously around the outer surface.

The GPW front fender is attached to the step on the lower edge with two bolts. The MB is attached by one.

The GPW firewall has an embossed reinforcing bar on the driver's side above the steering column.

The toolbox lid in the rear body of a GPW has ridges stamped into the cover. The MB has a solid piece. Also, the GPW has a rectangular depression of the latch, and the MB has a round one.

The battery space in the right inner fender is stamped on the GPW, and spot welded on the MB.

The footrests on a GPW have a triangular-shaped end bracket, and the MBs have a U-shaped end bracket.

The insulation webbing on the gas tank hold-down straps on a GPW is riveted on, where the MB's is stapled.

The inner fenders on the rear of a GPW just behind the shock mounts have vertical bars stamped in, and the MB does not.

6x6 adaptations of the standard jeep. There was a shortage of 3/4 ton trucks, and Willys hoped to capitalize on the shortage by building the MB-T, also known as the MT 6x6. As a vehicle, it was largely successful but was not adopted for use. Willys touted the 65 percent interchangeability of parts with the standardized jeep. A number of prototypes in several configurations were built in 1943, including 16 aircraft tugs complete with fifth wheels, an armored car, two or three 37mm gun carriers, and a cargo version.

A half-tracked version of the Willys jeep was built in 1943 for use as a snow tractor. The goal was to develop a way to rescue downed pilots flying over Canada and Alaska. A small number were built using the Willys designation of MT-ST and the military designation of T-28. Eventually, the M-7 snow tractor was developed by Allis-Chalmers that used Willys running gear but looked nothing like a jeep.

Almost Jeeps: Extra Light "Jeeps"

Crosley had been waiting in the wings with ideas during the jeep contract wars, but had no real chance of competing with the big boys. Crosley began to develop a light jeep, and an opportunity to present it soon appeared, thanks to the Army's fixation on extra light vehicles. Crosley submitted a light 4x4 called the Pup in 1942. It had a 38.3-ci, two-cylinder, air-cooled engine that cranked out a whopping 13.5 horsepower. Eventually, Crosley produced 36 of the 1,125-pound vehicles.

Field tests of the Crosleys gave the Army enough information to create updated specs and in 1943, several manufacturers, including Crosley, were asked to produce updated pilot models. W-O produced the MB-L and the WAC (Willys Air Cooled) rigs that provided the engineering basis for the later Mechanical Mules.

SWORDS INTO PLOWSHARES

DEVELOPING THE PEACETIME JEEPS

In April 1942, freelance designer Brooks Stevens had pitched the idea of a "Victory Car" based on the new jeep. Stevens' plan was for a small sedan-bodied car, with the same go-anywhere capabilities of the jeep and of similar dimensions. These ideas apparently never went beyond the discussion stage, but the idea of the jeep as a postwar workhorse and farmer's best friend did catch hold at Willys-Overland and became the company's working postwar goal and priority.

Everyone connected with the development of the military jeep knew there was a potential goldmine dividend in a peacetime variant. This was one reason for the gloves-off fighting. Less predictable at the outset were the bragging rights that went with being the major player in the jeep game. W-O fought hard because it needed to survive. As time went on, it was pretty clear to management that the jeep was W-O's ticket to fame and fortune.

The pilot model CJ-2s were the first true ground-up civilian jeeps. Although they incorporated many familiar military jeep parts, the body was specially made by American Central Manufacturing, and was considerably different from the GI units. The most notable visual feature of the early CJ-2s is the mounting of the spare tire, a situation that existed only for the first few vehicles. This is CJ-2-09, the second-earliest remaining civilian jeep and currently the only one that has been restored. It still wears the original bronze "JEEP" emblems, as well as the dash mounted "AGRIJEEP" data plate. This extremely rare jeep is owned by Fred Coldwell.

The civilian Jeep era began on April 13, 1942, when the United States Department of Agriculture (USDA) tested two jeeps at its Farm Tillage Machinery Laboratory in Auburn, Alabama. One jeep was a GPW borrowed from the Army Fourth Corps Quartermaster and the other a factory-fresh Willys MB. One of the test observers was Alabama Congressman Carter Manasco, who was a member of the subcommittee overseeing the disposal and conversion of war materiel to civilian use. Manasco had an idea to revive the postwar economy by giving departing GIs a surplus jeep for agricultural use: the 1940s' equivalent of the Civil War "40 acres and a mule" concept.

The USDA did not actually give the military jeep high marks as a pseudo-tractor. The report stated that, while the agency regarded the jeep as a good supplementary power source to run a power take-off (PTO), it was too low, too narrow, and geared too high for field use. It also needed a proper drawbar for plowing.

Not deterred, Manasco asked Willys in December 1943 to define its plans, if any, for the agricultural use of jeeps after the war. George Ritter, vice-president and general consul at Willys, responded in person, and with a lengthy report. He made it clear that Willys would not appreciate the government dumping military jeeps on the civilian market en masse and potentially killing the postwar Jeep's chances in the market. This exact scenario had occurred after World War I, when thousands of surplus Army trucks were sold dirt cheap or given away to state or municipal governments. A number of truck companies perished directly as a result.

Ritter also compiled data for Manasco listing the improvements needed to turn the military jeep into an agricultural workhorse. These included a rear PTO, lower axle gearing, improved cooling system, larger clutch, drawbar, and a stronger chassis. Ritter went on to specify that Willys' plans would result in a much improved and safer version of the jeep. Apparently the military jeep was good enough for GIs but not safe for civilians.

In the end, Willys pretty much got its way. Most jeeps sent overseas were not brought back and were either given to allied governments, sold where they lay, or as in the Pacific, where few sales outlets existed, disposed of by such means as dumping over the sides of ships or by using them for target practice.

The first civilian jeep at work is shown here during the spring 1944. Called the CJ-1, this pilot model was a rebuilt MB that was pulled off the production line and modified by the addition of a tailgate, lower axle ratios, a set of lower transfer case gears, drawbar, canvas half-top, and a few other agricultural accoutrements. This unit was quickly built for field tests while the CJ-2 models were being built. The bronze nameplate on the hood says "AGRIJEEP." Author/ Jeep historian Fred Coldwell recently unearthed photos of the CJ-1 and kindly allowed this one to be used here. *Fred Coldwell*

CJ-1: The First Civilian Jeep

The civilian Jeep project began in 1944 when W-O had some resources to spare beyond war-oriented production. Documentation of the exact timing is sketchy, but Fred Coldwell, author of *Selling the All American Wonder,* and Jeep expert Todd Paisley have studied the remaining documents extensively and determined that blueprints had been drawn up by February 1944 and a pilot model, dubbed the CJ-1 (the CJ was for "Civilian Jeep"), was up and running by May. It wore a cast-bronze hood emblem that said, "AGRIJEEP."

Although long doubted by some historians, the existence of a CJ-1 makes sense, given the gaps in the numbers, and Paisley and Coldwell managed to uncover written evidence and photos that prove the CJ-1's existence. It's clear the CJ-1 was an MB pulled off the line and modified with a tailgate, drawbar, civilian-type top, and a spare tire mounted on the passenger side. The CJ-1 also had lower gearing in the axles and transfer case, and most likely there were improvements in the clutch and cooling systems specified in the earlier Ritter report. There is proof that there was at least one CJ-1 pilot model.

CJ-2: Built for Tests

The CJ-2 project began concurrently with the CJ-1. The CJ-1 was essentially a quickly assembled test bed, but the CJ-2 prototypes were built from the ground up as civilian jeeps. The body, chassis, and much of the drivetrain were built especially for these units, even though many MB parts were also utilized.

There were at least 45 CJ-2 prototypes built, each built to test a certain upgrade or idea. Paisley and Coldwell have pieced together enough of the puzzle to note that CJ-2s were built in two distinct series: pilot models and standardized preproduction models. All the CJ-2s were alike in that they all had tailgates, 5.38 gears, lower transfer case gearing, T-90 column shift transmissions, and drawbars. Some had front brush guards and iron counterweights on the front bumpers. Many CJ-2s were equipped with PTOs and governors. Others mounted air compressors, post hole diggers, mowers, and various other equipment. Many CJ-2s mounted v-rib implement tires for traction in plowed fields.

Some of the pilot models have distinctive brass "JEEP" plaques mounted to the hood sides, windshield frame, and rear panel. The spare tire

The CJ-2s and early CJ-2As were extensively tested in the agricultural environment. This photo, taken in 1945, shows two CJs plowing in tandem. In the background is a CJ-2A with a trenching apparatus attached. During tests, Willys brought large groups of jeeps to a particular area, often a USDA facility, to work the ground and provide fodder for company photographers.

was mounted on the passenger side, forward of the rear wheel well. They used an MB-style grille with fixed headlights. The seats were standard MB but the dash was new and didn't include the MB glove box.

The standard CJ-2 series had "JEEP" stamped into the sheet metal of the hood sides and lower windshield frame. The early second series apparently used the AgriJeep nametags on the dash, but later ones did not. There were many detail differences, such as the spare tire being moved to behind the wheelwell. The last of the CJ-2s used what amounted to a standard CJ-2A body, including the large headlights and seven-slot grille. The CJ-2s proved that a civilian jeep could do the job in a civilian environment.

CJ-2A: Production CJ

Development of the production version of the CJ, later dubbed the CJ-2A, began in December 1944. Much of the development work took place on the CJ-2 prototypes, so it was a relatively quick process to get the model into production by July 1945. There were a large number of changes, the most visible of which was the civilian, seven-slot grille versus the old nine-slot military piece. The headlights were larger and mounted directly on the grille rather than behind it. The fuel filler was outside the body rather than under the seat. Many other changes make the CJ-2A a completely different animal from the CJ-2, or the military jeep.

A Willys test driver demonstrates how easy the Newgren hydraulic lift was to hook up to the 1946 CJ-2A. The lift allowed the plow blade to be hoisted for turning and to control depth. Several types of lifts were offered; Newgren and Monroe were two of the best known.

Here is your basic 1945 and early 1946 CJ. The earliest CJs used a column shift and still had the full-floating military axle. The military tool notches on the side of the body are also evident, as are the recessed front marker lights. These are all features that disappeared early in 1946.

You don't have to be observant to notice there is something odd with this Jeep. The 1951-only Jeep Tractor was stripped of nearly everything, including the lights and windshield. The idea was to offer a basic agriculture vehicle, but only a handful were sold, perhaps proving that you can go too basic. By the time this CJ-3A-based vehicle appeared, the country was in a recession, at war, and farmers were suffering from a drop in crop prices. These factors slowed sales of all Jeeps.

The CJ-2A was in rapid development for its first year. Early features of the CJ-2A that were later dropped include a column shift transmission, a full-float rear axle, recessed front marker lights, tool indents on the left body, and an MB-style exhaust system. By early 1947, the 2A had been standardized to a point where it would largely remain until it was phased out in 1949.

The CJ-2A was a better machine than its earlier GI brothers. It had a stronger chassis, a stronger T-90 Warner Gear three-speed replaced the military T-84, and it received a stronger version of the Model 18 transfer case with a 2.43:1 low range to replace the 1.97:1 of the military rigs. The suspension was improved to carry a 1,200-pound load. The CJ-2A was capable of a greater drawbar pull, a peak of nearly 2,300 pounds, versus the MB's 1,930 pounds.

The Go-Devil engine continued almost unchanged from the military engine until it received internal improvements in mid-1946 that included a new crankshaft, modified cylinder head, and a switch to a gear-driven camshaft instead of a chain-driven one. Power output was virtually the same.

Sales were very good, especially considering the number of cheap war-surplus jeeps on the market. For part of the 1945 and the full 1946 model years alone, more than 73,000 CJ-2As were sold. Total production of the CJ-2A was slightly more than 214,000. The CJ-2A departed just as a recession hit and caused an industrywide drop in sales.

CJ-3A: The CJ Refined

As the CJ neared the new decade, it was thought that a few upgrades were in order. They were not major ones, but in order to be able to announce a new model, W-O called the Jeep the CJ-3A. The most obvious change to the CJ-3A was the one-piece windshield and the vent just below it. Less noticeable were the body changes such as the reshaped rear wheelhouses that allowed the seat to move farther back for taller drivers. A new top arrangement also reduced "head slapping" for taller drivers.

Mechanically, the CJ-3A got a much stronger Spicer 44-2 rear axle, a better carburetor and fuel pump, and a higher rated clutch. The colors and accessory list changed a bit, but overall the CJ-3A was not really a major upgrade.

The CJ-2A and 3A were produced concurrently during the beginning of 1949. Along the same lines, the CJ-3A and 3B were also produced concurrently during 1953. Production was relatively low for the 3A, only a bit more than 138,000 units. The Korean War, a recession, and low crop prices all contributed to the low numbers.

Ag Specials: Farm Jeeps and Jeep Tractors

Willys-Overland had high hopes that the Universal Jeep could be marketed as the farmer's best friend. In fact, the company had bet a fair amount of resources on it. From the beginning, civilian Jeeps could be equipped to do virtually all the tasks of a small tractor and some the tractor couldn't.

During the CJ-3A run, W-O decided to market a special Farm Jeep package. Equipped with a hydraulic lift, drawbar, and governor, it was ready to work the furrowed fields. The Farm Jeeps were built from 1951 to 1953 on CJ-3A and CJ-3B chassis. While any Jeep could be equipped the same as a Farm Jeep, true Farm Jeeps had a special serial number prefix. In the case of the CJ-3A, it was 451-GC1 and 452-GC2 for the 1951 and 1952 models. The 1953 CJ-3B Farm Jeep wore a 453-GC2 prefix. Production of Farm Jeeps was spotty, occurring only during those years. Production information is equally spotty and conflicting, but one list shows 62 CJ-3A Farm Jeeps in 1951, 65 CJ-3A Farm Jeeps in 1952, and 85 CJ-3B Farm Jeeps in 1953.

A variation of the Farm Jeep was the Jeep Tractor. Built only in 1951 with the special serial number prefix of 451-GD1, this Jeep was a stripper in every sense. It didn't have a windshield or lights, and had only one seat. It was equipped with a governor, hydraulic lift, and a drawbar. It's unclear how many of these "go to work" special Jeeps were built, but it was likely only a handful.

Is it a Jeep or a bulldozer? Jim and Peg Marski's 1950 CJ-3A is outfitted for serious work. Up front, a Scheneker hydraulic plow is mounted, as well as a factory PTO-driven capstan winch. In back, a "Jeep-a-Trench" from the Auburn Machine Works is mounted. This Jeep has only 8,950 miles and all the equipment is operational. Even with the low mileage, the old Jeep is showing wear from use. Jeeps equipped with additions often bowed or hogged in the center, as this one has.

Half a Jeep is better than none. The Navy used these three-wheeled Jeep conversions as jet aircraft starting units on aircraft carriers for a number of years. A single undriven steering wheel was in the back and a non-steering driving axle was up front. This shot was taken in 1950 at the beginning of the Korean War. *National Archives*

The Station Sedan was the first full-boat luxo version of the six-cylinder Willys Wagons. Built only in 1948 and 1949, the Station Sedan only came as a two-wheeler.

CJ-4: The Lost CJ

The CJ-4 was the civilian offshoot from efforts to put the F-head four-cylinder in the military jeep chassis. The initial impetus was for a better military Jeep, but there was little doubt that a civvy variant would soon follow. The CJ-4 pilot was built in 1950 and combined a CJ-3A with the F-head and a new front wrap. The result was not unpleasant in appearance and was certainly a better performer than the L-head-powered Jeeps. What slowed its development was the rationing of certain raw materials needed for the Korean War. By the time resources were freed up, a much simpler adaptation was conceived in the form of the CJ-3A. Only one CJ-4 pilot model was built, probably concurrent with the military CJ-4M.

CJ-3B: Last of the W-O CJs

The CJ-3B was a simple adaptation of the CJ-3A that put the more powerful F-head engine into the Universal chassis at a low cost. The result was a great performing flatfender, but one that earned some raised eyebrows for its unconventional look. Called the CJ-4A in its developmental state, it emerged in January 1953 as the CJ-3B. Commonly called the "High-Hood" Jeep, it was built under the old W-O nameplate for only a few short months before Kaiser's late April purchase of Willys-Overland.

Besides the more powerful F-head engine and the bodywork, the CJ-3B was much like the CJ-3A. They were produced concurrently through the majority of 1953. The extra power gave the 3B a serious performance edge over its ancestors, but it was an easy upgrade to produce. The carryover of parts from the earlier models was over 90 percent.

By the time the CJ-3B was in production, plans for a new Jeep, the CJ-5, were well under way. It's likely that the CJ-3B was considered an interim model that would be dropped once the new Jeep was established. Nobody would have guessed that the little Jeep that has worn such names as "The Ugly Duckling" would become the most enduring Jeep of all time.

Station Wagons: A New Idea

The Station Wagon was another gem from the fertile mind of Brooks Stevens, a master of innovation on a budget. Development began in 1944, just as Charles "Cast Iron Charlie" Sorenson took over as president. At the time, Stevens and others were working on the postwar Willys car designs. Sorenson put the kibosh on that, noting that a postwar Willys car was just another car. He made the company goal by building a vehicle that capitalized on the wartime jeep and seized a unique place in the market. Car production did not resume until 1952 when Sorenson was no longer president.

When the pickup was introduced in 1947, it was available in two- and four-wheel drive. The 4x2s were available in half- and one-ton ratings, but all the 4x4s were one-tonners, as is this 1948. *Jane L. Barry, Willys America*

July 1946 brought the new idea to the Willys line. It was part car and part truck but W-O called it the All-Steel Station Wagon. At first glance, one would be forgiven to remark, "Oh, a woody!" It did look like the woody but was all stamped steel. This wagon holds the record for being the first fully steel-bodied station wagon built in America.

With the grille being the most recognizable element of the jeep, Stevens used it as a starting point to create the Station Wagon. The same basic design was easily adapted into a panel or a pickup. Some problems were found in the manufacture of the unique body panels because some of the automotive panel makers who were consulted balked at the complicated molds. Sorenson's solution was to bypass the automotive specialists altogether and use a manufacturer that normally stamped out sheet metal for washing machines.

Sorenson had a powerful and sometimes abrasive personality, and his ideas on the future of Willys were not necessarily agreed upon among Willys'

Specialty conversions of the Willys truck line were common. This 1947 4x4 had been set up to carry explosives. It also mounts a custom brush guard and a big Ramsey winch.

When ordered with all the goodies, the early Station Wagons like this 1947 4-63 could be quite flashy. The paint scheme mimicked the woody station wagons built by other manufacturers, but was without the upkeep and rapid deterioration of a true woody. To 1948, only a 63-horsepower version of the L-head four was available. In that year, the 148-ci six made its debut with a 6-horsepower boost. The interior appointments were comparable to the medium-level trimmed cars. A single side facing seat in the cargo area was optional.

other ruling board members. Reports of open boardroom warfare abounded. Ward Canaday, the financial wizard of the company, finally had enough and replaced Sorenson with James Mooney in January 1946. This happened shortly before Sorenson's baby, the All-Steel Station Wagon, made its debut in July. Mooney put W-O's car plans back onto the agenda, but time has shown that Sorenson's ideas for the future success of W-O in the postwar world were more astute in many ways than Mooney's.

The first Willys Station Wagons were all 4x2s. The front suspension was called the Planadyne and was a revamp of the Barney Roos design used on Studebakers in the 1930s. It consisted of a transverse leaf spring, with the lower end of a spindle attached. The upper end of the spindle was connected to an A-arm that was attached to the chassis rail at the other end. The powertrain was built around the Go-Devil engine and used drivetrain pieces from the same manufacturer that built the jeep's running gear. The vehicle was built on a 104-inch wheelbase, and the chassis was designated the 4-63

For 1950, the Willys trucks lost the flat front and received the V-nose treatment the vehicles would keep for the rest of the run. This 1950 4-73 truck was also equipped with a high compression version F-head four (hence the yellow painted head) that increased the power to up to 72 horsepower. This low mileage rig was once used by the LaVeta, Colorado, fire department and is now part of the Jim and Peg Marski Jeep collection.

The 1948 to early 1950 Jeepster VJs shared the flat-nosed front end. Jim and Peg Marski's 1949 is resplendent in Luzon Red and black. Today the phaeton-style top is quaint, but at the time it was a throwback to a true convertible.

(4-cylinder, 63 horsepower), to which the body type was added, such as 4-63 Station Wagon or 4-63 Panel Delivery.

W-O had established a limited prewar reputation with the four-cylinder Go-Devil engine. The company soon learned that more was needed, both from a driver's point of view and for bragging rights. Late in 1947, a Roos-designed six-cylinder engine made its debut for the 1948 model year. This 148-ci "Lightning" unit was the smallest displacement six ever offered in America. With only 70 horsepower, it was a very small step up the performance ladder, but it was a smooth, high-revving engine for the day.

Other big news for 1948 was the introduction of the Station Sedan. This was an upscale six-cylinder special that featured a deluxe interior with many unique features. Outside, the Station Sedan was recognized by its stainless steel T-bar grille piece and basket weave appliqué in the panels under the windows. It was the most plush Willys unit of the time, and was perhaps the most plush Station Wagon Willys ever built, but only 5,106 units were built to March 1949.

The most significant moment in Willys Station Wagon history was the introduction of the 4x4 models in 1949. The 4x4-63 models were almost identical to the 4x2s, with a few changes in the firewall and floor to accommodate the 4x4 equipment. Only the four-cylinder engine was available and

the "uprated" 63-horsepower Go-Devil moved the 4x4 Wagon with the authority of Barney Fife. A little help came early in 1950, when the F-head "Hurricane" four was introduced. In high compression form, it had more power than the 148-ci six. With the new engine, the model designation changed to 4-73.

A bigger six was introduced in 1950 for the 6-73 4x2 models. The 75-horsepower, 161-ci L-head six had a bit more grunt than its modest power figure would indicate. This L-head didn't last long and was replaced by an F-head version of the 161-ci engine that made 90 horsepower. Again, it was available only in 4x2 station wagons and panels, but the equipped wagons used a 685 model designation. This engine was available in 4x2s to 1955, which was well into the Kaiser era.

Most of the major changes in the Station Wagon and Sedan Delivery lines came after the Kaiser purchase in 1953. This date generally marks a gradual transition toward the 4x4 models that gave the company a unique spot in the market.

Pickups: Willys Workhorse

The Willys-Overland pickups made their debut in May 1947, but unlike the Station Wagons, they were available immediately as both two- and

The Sedan Delivery or Panel Delivery, the nomenclature depends on the year, was a small but important part of the early lineup. This 1951 4-73 two-wheeler predates the Kaiser takeover and is a part of the Paul Barry/Willys America collection.

Jeepsters built after April 1950 received the same V-nose treatment as the rest of the Willys line. They also were given the more powerful F-head engine.

four-wheel-drive units. The 4x2s came as half- and one-ton units, while the 4x4s were all rated as one-tons. Until 1949, the trucks were a column-shift three-speed and the four-cylinder engine was the only engine available in the W-O era. The 4x2s used a beam-type axle.

The trucks had a wide variety of options and configurations. They were available as pickups, stake beds, flatbeds, with utility bodies or wrecker apparatus, to name just a few of the factory options. The aftermarket listed even more. Except for a few special cases, the 4x2 version of the pickup was dropped after 1951. The 4x4s were more popular and generally useful. As with the Station Wagons, there is more to tell about the pickups in the Kaiser era.

JEEPSTER: THE WILLYS SPORTS CAR

The Brooks Stevens-designed Jeepster made its debut in April 1948 as W-O's answer to a budding sports car craze. Increased prosperity had allowed many middle class families the option of a second car and market analysis pointed to a "fun" car as a likely sale. Codenamed the VJ, the Jeepster was all of that. It was a low-slung four-seater ragtop with much of the styling taken from the Station Wagon models. It shared the same flat-nosed and recognizable Jeep front end. The Jeepster was one of the last, if not the last, American automobile to use side curtains instead of windows. Although it is called a "roadster" or "touring car" by some, it is more accurately termed a "phaeton."

Willys-Overland was willing to take risks. The development of an aluminum-bodied vehicle started in early 1948. Two pilot models, commonly known as Alcoa Coupes, were built in a business coupe form. They were a collaboration between Willys, Goodyear Aircraft, and ALCOA. Pilot number one was based on a 4-63 VJ chassis, and pilot number two was based on a later 6-73 chassis. They appear rather tail heavy, but the trunk was big enough for an embalmed caribou. Number two received a slightly altered front-end treatment, while the first unit kept the traditional VJ nose. The project was dropped after 1951, when steel prices returned to normal.

Fire conversions of the Willys truck were a common occurrence. The all-wheel drive was helpful in getting them closer to a fire or a source of water. Paul Barry's 1952 Willys "Ranger" fire truck was converted by Mobile Fire Apparatus, Inc., and features a 500-gallon-per-minute pump, a 150-gallon water tank, and a 150-foot hose reel. Since the pump is PTO driven, the engine can be easily overheated while the truck is stationary, so the Ranger was also supplied with a heat exchanger that used incoming pump water for cooling.

Unlike the Willys pickups and wagons, the VJ was never available in four-wheel drive. By the standards of the time, the Jeepster was sporty, at least in appearance. Powered by the Go-Devil engine, the 2,600-pound rig was "acceleration challenged" in a major way. In the first year, only the 63-horsepower four was available, but midway through 1949, the 148-ci Lightning six-cylinder was introduced as an option in the Jeepster. In 1950, the Jeepsters received the same engine upgrades as the rest of the line, the F-head Hurricane and the 161-cid six. Neither turned the VJ into a hot rod, but at least acceleration was not an embarrassment.

With only 20,353 units produced over a little more than two years, the VJ Jeepster was not regarded as a success. Most historians attribute this to the phaeton configuration. In an era where the weather-tight convertible was still a relatively new phenomenon, a step back to the earlier days of wetness, drafts, and poor visibility was not appealing to many buyers, even if the Jeepster had an attractive flair and a superb pedigree. Willys ceased producing Jeepsters late in 1950 and leftovers were retailed as 1951 models.

EXPERIMENTAL: ALCOA COUPE

An almost-milestone for Jeep and the automotive world in general was the Alcoa Coupe. Only two pilot models were built, but they represented a big shift in thinking that came fairly close to reality. Land Rover is often and rightly credited for its foresight in developing and introducing aluminum-bodied utility vehicles in 1948, but it's interesting to note that Willys-Overland was hot on the heels of the idea at nearly the same time in history.

The idea of an aluminum Jeep came sometime early in 1948 and it was as much a response to high steel prices as it was an idea for a lightweight car. Letters hint that James Mooney, then president of W-O, might have been the instigator, but it's clear that Barney Roos was also behind it and did much of the ramrodding.

The project was a three-way partnership with the American Aluminum Company of America (Alcoa), Goodyear Aircraft Corporation, and Willys-Overland Motors. The goal was to develop the techniques needed to produce automotive bodies in aluminum. The costs of the bodies were to be divided three ways, and Willys supplied two Jeepster chassis, one 134-ci 4-63 four-cylinder variant and one 161-ci 6-73 variant. Both units were completed and tested in 1951, and it was found that the 11 percent loss in weight added greatly to acceleration, and the lowered center of gravity improved handling.

The project was shelved in 1951, when a massive cost overrun at Goodyear Aircraft took the wind out of their sales (pun intended). By that time sheet steel prices had stabilized and eliminated much of the motivation to continue. Roos was an enthusiastic supporter right to the end.

CHAPTER 5

1949–1965

BRUSH WARS
AND
GARRISON DUTY

MILITARY JEEPS AFTER WORLD WAR II

Today, the building of military vehicles has become a highly specialized but very small part of the automotive market. Where mainstream builders once diverted a fair amount of attention to military vehicles, the market is now left to niche builders. It's interesting to note that one of the larger of these, AM General, builder of the world-famous Humvee, is a direct descendant of the great military vehicle builder once known as Willys-Overland.

Military Jeep development did not end after World War II. It slowed somewhat, but in the early days at least, it still drove civilian Jeep development to a large degree. The most common type of civilian utility Jeep, the ubiquitous CJ-5 "round fender" Jeep and its progeny, the CJ-6, CJ-7, CJ-8, and CJ-10, all came from the same source, the military M-38A1 (MD) Jeep.

The American ground forces underwent a great change of focus after World War II. Gone were the ex-Cavalry and Great War stick-in-the-muds. The motor vehicle had finally gained total acceptance and dominance. With America's newfound prosperity and stature, the pace of advance in civilian automotive technology increased rapidly, and much of this new stuff came to the MVs of the period.

The M-151 was developed by Ford in the early 1950s and went into production in 1959. The M-151 was produced by Ford, Willys Motors, and AM General. It was produced on and off in several variants until 1985. This is the M-151A1, the second generation M-151. Jon Huddlestan's vehicle is a 1968 Model and has been upgraded with the Rollover Protection System (ROPS). The M-151A1 went into production in 1965 and is most recognizable by the small marker lights on the fenders, blackout lights on the grille panel, vacuum wipers, and split windshield.

A NEW BUILDUP

Not much occurred in the military Jeep world until the late 1940s. The ground forces' fleet of World War II jeeps was aging and the lessons of war dictated changes to the quarter-ton role. Improvements in communication created a better compatibility with military radios, and a change to 24-volt electrical systems was made so that all vehicles had the potential to power the same radio sets. Light artillery had progressed to the point where a 105mm recoilless rifle could be mounted on the jeep, giving the vehicle great offensive capabilities.

One continuing thrust was standardization. As much as possible, the military wanted standard parts across the board. Small parts such as instruments, lighting, batteries, charging systems, and so on were standardized to cover as much of the vehicle inventory as possible, from quarter-tons to 10-tons and beyond.

Before long, the military came to Willys asking for a new Jeep incorporating all the changes needed for the new American ground forces. Willys was still flush from war profits and an early boost in the civilian market, but the company still considered the military a bread-and-butter market and their attitude was "can-do!" Through the 1950s and 1960s, Willys, which later became Kaiser-Willys, rolled a number of innovations off the military vehicle assembly lines, as well as some of their standard workmanlike fare.

M-38: A Heavy Jeep

The Willys Model MC, known to the military as the M-38, started development in December 1948 as project 5200. The goal was to provide a quarter-ton with improved military characteristics and performance over the earlier MB. The new set of requirements included a higher payload (max of 1,200 pounds versus 800 for the MB), provision for the easy installation of a fording kit, provision for fitting a winch, standardized instruments and small parts, radio suppressed ignition, and a 24-volt electrical system. Willys determined that its new civilian CJ-3A came close, so it became the basis for the new GI rig. It had a stronger drivetrain and many improved features over the World War II rig.

Seven pilot and prototype vehicles were built for tests, and it was found that with all the new equipment, the GI Jeep had gained some weight. The new MC was 300 pounds heavier than the MB and 550 pounds heavier than the CJ-3A. In tests it was found that performance was moderately impaired with the vehicle lightly loaded and severely impaired with a capacity load. It's no surprise, since the engine was still essentially the same old 60-horsepower Go-Devil flathead of World War II fame. A partial answer was found in a gear ratio change. The military had specified 4.88:1 gear ratios. A change to the civilian 5.38:1 ratios brought performance up to acceptable levels, but period tests show the Army still regarded performance as barely adequate.

The M-38 started production in September 1950. It saw some combat in the Korean War and began replacing the tired World War II jeeps. Production for the M-38 ended rather quickly under U.S. contracts, with the last unit leaving the assembly line in July 1952. A total of just more than 62,000 were built for U.S. contracts. A few thousand more were built at the Canadian Willys subsidiary and an export contract in 1955 added another 3,380 units.

CJ-V35/U: The Navy Jeep

This adaptation of the CJ-3A actually started development eight months earlier than the MC. The Navy had requested a military Jeep for use by beachmasters on amphibious operations. It needed deep-water fording capacities and the ability to run some specialized radio equipment. Willys presented the CJ-V35/U ("U" for underwater), which was essentially a civilian CJ-3A with a waterproofed engine and drivetrain as well as a PTO-driven 12-volt generator between the seats for powering the radios. The main vehicle's electrical system remained 6 volts. Later, a 24-volt generator replaced the 12-volt unit when military radios all changed over to that voltage. Only 1,000 V-35/U units were produced from March to June 1950. From the available records, it appears that much of the M-38's fording equipment came from the early research done on the CJ-V35/U.

Missing Links: Flat-Fenders to Round-Fenders

In the midst of the struggles over the MC's lack of performance in 1949, Willys let military representatives drive a Willys Station Wagon equipped with the new, yet unreleased F-head engine. Called the "Hurricane," this new four-cylinder engine had 9 to 13 more horsepower (depending on compression ratio) than the standard Go-Devil L-head. This engine was an adaptation of the L-head block and had been in development since 1947. The testers were impressed enough to inquire about stuffing this engine into a quarter-ton. Willys was thinking along the same lines and went to work producing a test vehicle in June 1949.

The L- and F-head engines were similar, but the one major difference was height. The F-head was 4 inches taller and required more hood clearance. The cowl was raised the required amount, and the nose piece was changed to fit a new, taller hood. The pilot model offered the first glimpse of the rounded hood later made famous on the CJ-5.

The pilot model F-head Jeep made its debut in 1950, with the earliest known photos taken in August. It was tested against World War II-era jeeps, M-38 Jeeps and a CJ-3A, and outperformed them all. This pilot model led to the CJ-4M and M-38E1 prototypes as well as the CJ-4MA. All of these eventually

The pilot models of the MC were not very different in appearance from the production M-38. Underneath, however, there were some differences. The test MCs used 4.88:1 axle ratios that, combined with the extra weight and larger 7.00-16 tires, made them much slower than the World War II jeeps. The addition of 5.38:1 axle ratios in the production models brought acceleration back up to acceptable levels, but still not as good as the World War II rigs. This unit was pilot model number 7 and had a Ramsey winch and the fording kit installed.

became building blocks for the M-38A1 (MD). What's interesting about this group of test vehicles is that they evolved from flat-fenders, through some stylized flat-fenders to the round-fenders we have come to know and love in the CJs.

M-38A1: The Last Real Military Jeep?

Beginning in 1951 under project number 6600, the model MD came directly from the previous efforts to install the F-head into the CJ. The M-38A1 is widely regarded as the best Willys military Jeep ever built, and many have called it the last "real" military Jeep. The M-38A1 began production in April 1952 and continued until 1968. The U.S. Army contracts ended in 1957 with a total of 82,000 produced units, but the U.S.M.C. continued to purchase MDs at least as late as 1964. Many MDs were exported to military organizations all over the world and many still serve. The numbers show that slightly more than 104,000 vehicles were eventually built.

The M-38 used standardized military switches and instruments, and featured a small glove box. One of the few differences to note between 1950/1951 and 1952 models is that the earlier units have the data plates screwed directly to the dash. The later models have the data plates screwed to a separate plate that is screwed to the dash. This is a 1951 M-38.

The resemblance to the civilian CJ-3A can be seen but there are also many differences to note. The windshield vent is permanently closed via brackets, there are headlamp guards, and the grille panel is mounted on hinges for easy power plant removal. There are also recovery shackles on the bumper, and the right body sill is notched for tools in the opposite position of the MB/GPW. Gary Wirth's 1951 M-38 is complete with a dummy .50-caliber machine gun on a pedestal mount and a radio, as well as a set of nonoriginal locking hubs.

There were a number of variants of the M-38A1, including the M-170 long-wheelbase ambulance you'll read about later. Some of the simplest variants that show up are the 1,232 units with 6-volt electrical systems. More elaborate were the M-38A1C models that mounted a recoilless rifle. Besides being beefed up to carry the gun and ammo, it had a notched windshield for the gun tube and special ammunition racks. A potent variation was the M-38A1D that was equipped with the Davy Crockett launcher. This weapons system could fire conventional or tactical nuclear projectiles. It was deployed briefly in 1962, but was withdrawn from front-line service because of a natural reluctance to placing nuclear weapons in the hands of junior officers.

The M-38A1 provided the basis for the civilian CJ-5, which made its debut in 1954. It remained in service into the 1980s and there may still be a few lurking in

Restorers crave to be different. Ray Shumate went Navy with his M-38 restoration, painting his 1952 up as a 3rd Fleet Jeep attached to an aviation squadron. Some owners get quite creative in reproducing a specific vehicle or era.

This obviously retouched photo depicts the "missing link" between the flat-fender and rounder fender military Jeeps. Known alternately as the CJ-4M or the M-38E1, this 1950/51 pilot model brought the F-head to the military Jeep line. The fenders, cowl, grille, and windshield are obviously unique to this line of vehicles, but the hood is clearly recognizable as the hoods that were fitted to later M-38A1s. This vehicle is a direct ancestor of the M-38A1 and CJ-5.

government service somewhere. The MD was replaced by the M-151 in service starting in 1960, but many military units were reluctant to abandon the earlier jeep.

M-170: The Mercy Jeep

The MDA, or M-170, was designed as a front-line ambulance. It was based on the M-38A1, but had a longer, 101-inch wheelbase, a larger fuel tank, and more room to carry patients due to its extra length. The payload remained the same as the M-38A1, at 800 pounds cross country and 1,200 pounds highway, but it was designed to carry three patients in litters or six ambulatory patients. The MDA started production in late 1953 and was periodically built in small numbers up to 1967. In all, 4,800 units were produced. The later civilian CJ-6 was based on the M-170.

Bobcat: Jeep Light

The resounding cry from the ground forces from the mid-1940s was that they wanted their jeeps smaller and lighter. The goal was air portability, either via fixed wing, parachute, or helicopter. Willys had previously responded with World War II-era concepts like the MB-L, a stripped version of the MB. In the early 1950s, the answer was the Model BC, also known as the Aero-Jeep or Bobcat. Built under the guidance of Mike Ordorica, Willys' Chief military engineer at the time, the vehicle was a combination of the lightest off-the-shelf Willys parts and some specially made aluminum pieces, including an aluminum version of the L-head engine and special aluminum transmission and transfer case castings. The body was mostly aluminum, created on modified steel sheet metal molds. The

Another missing link is the CJ-4MA, a stretched ambulance version of the CJ-4M. This vehicle was photographed in late March 1951 and it led directly to the M-170 front-line ambulance, as well as the CJ-6.

The M-38A1, or Willys Model MD, became a military standard for many years. Production began in April 1952 for U.S. Army contracts. This factory photo depicts a later model that was photographed in 1960. Later models, 1954 up, can be easily discerned by the full-width bumper, the lack of grill hinges, and a single strap holding down the battery box.

result was a 1,500-pound machine that moved like a jackrabbit. A number of prototypes were built and successfully tested, but the design never went into production.

M-422: Almost a Jeep

The Mighty Mites were not built by Willys, but there are a couple of connections, besides the general layout, that make them worthy of inclusion. The production vehicles were built by the Nash Kelvinator branch of the newly formed American Motors, and one of the principal designers was Harold Crist, of the 1940 Bantam jeep fame. Crist was working with the Mid-America Research Company (MARCO) in the early 1950s when it responded to a Marine Corps request for a lightweight, air portable, jeeplike vehicle.

The MM-100 emerged in 1953 and became known as the Mighty Mite. It was an aluminum-bodied unit with an air-cooled Porsche engine, inboard brakes and fully independent suspension. The Mighty Mite weighed only 1,500 pounds.

The basic design tested well and further development was handed off to American Motors. By 1960, a unit was approved for production. It differed in many ways from the original, with a more powerful V-4 air-cooled aluminum engine and a different drivetrain. The aluminum body and independent suspension were the same, but the unit gained some weight and grew to 1,800 pounds.

Herb Huddle's restored 1952 M-38A1 is painted to depict a Marine Corps vehicle. Note the narrow front bumper, grill hinges, and battery box lid held down with four straps and wing nuts that are the earmarks of an early MD. Marine Corps Jeeps also had some minor differences from U.S. Army units, and the most noticeable difference was the tie-down rings at the rear.

WHAT'S ALL THIS "M" STUFF?

Shortly after World War II began, the ground forces adopted a complete classification system for all equipment. The system changed slightly over the years, but is still in use today. Each piece of equipment is placed into a category, and each is given an M-number ("M" for "Model"). There might be an M-3 light tank, M-3 motorcycle, and M-3 footlocker, each within its own category of equipment.

If a significant production upgrade of the basic unit is developed, it would be given a designation of M-2A1. If another development occurs, it becomes an M-2A2, and so on. Small scale or field modifications might receive a B, C, or D suffix; for example, a limited numbers modification of our M2 vehicle might be known as the M-2A2B1.

Experimental designations are different. In the World War II era, experimental rigs had a "T" number (T-6 tractor). Experimental classifications changed after World War II to "X." For example, if a newly designed experimental light tank is developed, it would be known as the XM-4. As soon as the new XM-4 is accepted for use, it becomes the M-4. A similar situation exists with upgrades. If some modification or improvement is concocted for the M-4, that improvement must be tested. Until the modification is approved, the vehicle is designated the M-4E1, or M-4A1E1.

Two versions of the Mighty Mite were produced for the U.S. Marine Corps: the M-422 and the M-422A1. The latter unit was 6.5 inches longer than the former. Fewer than 4,000 units were produced of both vehicle types. They saw service in Vietnam and elsewhere, but were being phased out by the early 1970s, since the need for lightweight vehicles diminished as helicopter capacity increased.

M-151 M.U.T.T.: No Dog

The M-151 was another jeeplike vehicle that was developed by another manufacturer but was eventually produced by Willys, and later AM General. The goal of this vehicle was to simplify and modernize the quarter-ton concept. Development began in 1951 under a contract that gave the government all licensing rights to every part of the vehicle, whether it was newly developed or off the shelf. That meant that even the subcontractors involved in supplying previously licensed parts had to allow the government the freedom to put the manufacture of the part out for bid. The task was taken up by the Ford Ordnance Vehicle Project Department and a prototype, the XM-151, was created in 1952.

The result was a unibody type vehicle called the Military Utility Tactical Truck (M.U.T.T.) with a fully independent coil spring suspension, inboard brakes (later dropped), a 71 horsepower OHV engine, four-speed transmission, and single-speed transfer case. It was lighter, lower, and more fuel efficient than the M-38A1. The government adopted the design, and put the manufacture of the units up for open bid. Ford came first in 1959 with a run of 4,050, and again in 1961 with 13,124 vehicles. Willys got into the act in 1962 and built 24,508 units. Ford built nearly 100,000 units from 1964 to 1968. AM General jumped in during 1971 to build another 34,000-plus jeeps, and after that, it was an all-AM General deal. The M-151 was gradu-

ally replaced by the Humvee starting in the early 1980s, and the last few M-151s were built in 1985 for an export contract. The assembly line in South Bend, Indiana, was shut down the same year. The last versions of the M-151 are still used in limited numbers within the U.S. military organization.

There were three distinct evolutions of the M-151: the original unit (1960–1965), the M-151A1 (1965-1970), and the M-151A2 (1970–1985). The original M-151 rear suspension was flawed, and in certain cornering situations, it could cause the vehicle to roll over. This was preventable by altering driving technique—specifically, by slowing down. Military organizations tried to solve the problem by driver training, but soon realized that trying to slow down testosterone-charged young men was an impossibility. In the end, they directed that the manufacturer make an alteration to the rear suspension to make the vehicles less rollover prone. This led to the M-151A2.

Starting in 1970, a revised suspension was introduced on the A2 models, as well as a number of other improvements. Other safety improvements followed, and in 1988, at the end of the M-151 timeline, the Rollover Protection System (ROPS) was introduced, consisting of a full roll cage, improved seat belts, and safety nets. Older M-151s still in service were retrofitted with this new safety feature.

While a small number of M-151s found their way onto the surplus market beginning in 1970, the government soon decided M-151s could not be sold intact due to lack of DOT certification and safety concerns. To prevent them from being used on the highway, the basic structure had to be destroyed and the remains were sold as scrap. At first, the vehicles were cut in half. When enterprising civilians began welding them back together, the Army began cutting the body into quarters. These days the body structure must be

The M-170, or Willys Model MDA, was designed as a front-line ambulance. It was used for many years and was built, on and off, from 1953 to 1967. It was nearly identical to the M-38A1, but had a 101-inch wheelbase, a larger, 20-gallon fuel tank, and could carry three patients in litters. Keith Buckley's M-170 is an original restoration, except for the modern Goodyear tires and Warn hubs. These were both installed to enhance driving the vehicle.

The M-38A1D was the most powerful jeep of all time. In the early 1960s a number of M-38A1s were retrofitted with the Davy Crockett launcher. This unique weapon could fire conventional or nuclear-tipped rounds at ranges of up to 2.5 miles.

The M-151A2 appeared in 1970 and was the last variant of the M-151 series. It featured a major workover of the rear suspension, combination blackout/turn signal/marker lights, electric wipers, and many other improvements. This 1971 was built by AM General and is owned by Ron Beyes. It is configured as a Military Police unit.

crushed or shredded to prevent enterprising civilian buyers from putting them back on the road.

The M-151 chassis was used for a number of variants. One was the M-718 or M-718A1C front-line ambulance and another was the M-825 or M-151A1C, which mounted a recoilless rifle.

M-606: Export Only

The M-606 was an export idea that modified standard civilian Jeeps into military vehicles by the addition of Olive Drab paint (OD, the standard military lusterless paint), blackout lights, a military style trailer receptacle, and a military-style pintle hitch. They were a cost-effective alternative to a full-blown spec-built military rig. The M-606 units were most often sold to foreign military organizations with limited funds.

The first M-606 units were based on the CJ-3B. When that model was phased out in 1968, the M-606A2 that was based on the CJ-5 replaced it. The M-606A2 was sold up through 1972. Another variation of the CJ-5 was also offered and called the M-606A3. It was the same unit as the M-606A2 but with a 24-volt electrical system. Some of all the M-606 variations were sold to the U.S. government for use on American military bases overseas.

M-715: Gladiator in Olive Drab

The M-715 was the truck that came out of nowhere and ended Dodge's 27-year lock on the three-quarter-ton military truck market. It also managed to beat a fabulous offering from GM on cost. The unit was based on the civilian Jeep Gladiator pickup chassis but assembled from the ultra-heavy-duty parts catalog and rated for 1 1/4 tons (called a "five-quarter" by GIs). The unit made its debut in March 1966 and was in production from January 1967 until May 1969, with over 30,500 vehicles produced. About 22,000 of the M-715s were cargo trucks.

Several variations of the basic chassis were built, including the M-725 ambulance and the M-726 utility-bodied truck. The Jeeps were good trucks overall, but the Dodge M-37 truck was generally preferred by the GIs. The M-715 suffered from a reputation problem because of poor engine reliability. Most of the bad rep came from the early days of the 230-ci overhead-cam six that made its debut in 1962. Although out of civilian production since 1965, the military variant of the OHC 230 had a pretty good record.

Platform Vehicles: What a Concept!

Willys played a big role in perfecting the platform vehicle for military use. A platform vehicle is simply a cargo bed on wheels, with a single, barely adequate driver's seat. They are simple, light, and easy to transport. Willys was competing for an extra-light quarter-ton contract during World War II when the platform vehicle idea was conceived. Two vehicles that came out of this project were the WAC (Willys Air Cooled) and the similar Jungle Burden Carrier. The latter idea became the XM-274 "Mechanical Mule" prototype of 1951. The M-274 was approved for production in 1956.

The half-ton rated M-274s came in several variations. The earliest M-274 and M-274A1 used a four-cylinder Willys engine and were built by

The M-151 series has been fitted with a number of heavy weapons, the TOW antitank missile included. Units equipped like this M-151A2C are designed to "shoot and scoot."

The early M-151 rear suspension was the source of some problems. The control arms pivoted along the centerline of the vehicle. In certain situations, the arms allowed the rear wheels to tuck in and cause the vehicle to roll. The improved system made its debut in 1970 M-151A2s and pivots at nearly 90 degrees of the centerline. This maintains safe suspension geometry. This rig also has a ROPS kit installed.

A variation of the M-151 is the M-718 field ambulance. It replaced the M-170 in front-line service. This is an M-718A1 version and it can carry up to four patients. Except for the ambulance accoutrements and heavier spring rates, it's identical to the standard M-151A1.

Willys until 1964. The M-274A1 used a Continental-Hercules two-cylinder engine and was built by Bowen-McLaughlin-York. The A3 and A4 models were simply rebuilt/upgraded earlier units. The M-274A5 was built by Bailfield Industries beginning in 1965. The last units built were in 1970. The older M-274s were retired in the early 1970s.

In the late 1950s, Willys came up with a variation of the platform vehicle. It was called the Convertible Mule or the Commercial Mule, and was designated as the XM-443. The unit was bigger than the M-274 and rated for a three-quarter-ton load. The "convertible" aspect related to the removable body panels. The unit could be stripped to a bare platform, or equipped with various panels to give it a fully or partially enclosed body. A couple of variations on the theme were developed, including a civilian variant, but the project died in the early 1960s.

M-676: Forward Thinking

When Willys introduced Forward Control in 1956, it had hoped its new concept in light trucks would be wildly successful. It didn't quite sell as well as expected, but in the early 1960s the Marine Corps was enticed to try a few special variants. The Air Force and Army bought some as well.

Besides the standard FC-170 pickup platform, Willys developed a crew-cab variant, a van-bodied carryall, and an ambulance. Once the models were accepted, they were designated M-676, M-677, M-678, and M-679, respectively. Most of the M-series forward controls were powered by a unique modular diesel engine made by Cerlist. It was a 170-ci, three-cylinder, two-stroke diesel with a blower. Some were equipped with hardened injection pumps and were suitable as multi-fuel engines. Complete production information is not available, but around 3,000 units of all types were produced.

The M-422 Mighty Mite was only used by the USMC and was produced from 1960 to 1963. With a mostly aluminum body, an air-cooled aluminum V4 engine, and a high-tech independent suspension, it was ahead of its time in many ways. The Mighty Mite was a successful performer but by the time it was produced, its intended role as a lightweight air-portable vehicle was largely made obsolete by more-powerful helicopters. The M-422 was the short-wheelbase variant, with a 64.5-inch wheelbase, an overall length of 107 inches, and a curb weight of 1,700 pounds. This restored 1960 Mighty Mite belongs to Don Haas.

The M-422A1 was an enlarged version of the Mighty Mite that appeared immediately after the first version. It had a 71-inch wheelbase, an overall length of 113 inches, and a curb weight of 1,780 pounds. They are virtually identical to the M-422 except for the dimensions. In fact, some of the "short" ones were converted into the "long" ones. The extra rib in the body behind the door opening is the giveaway of the larger Mighty-Mite. Fred LaPerriere restored this vehicle.

Barney Roos himself was responsible for many of the designs for the M-274 Mechanical Mule, having personally worked on the project as far back as 1944. The early versions of this platform vehicle were powered by a 52-ci four-cylinder Willys-Continental air-cooled engine. Later versions used a two-cylinder engine of nearly the same power and displacement. Mules went into production in 1957 and a total of about 9,300 were built in various configurations and by various manufacturers to 1970. The Mule could carry an honest half-ton of cargo.

Left
The M-715 military Gladiator breezed by the competition with a combination of price and value. From 1967–1969, some 30,500 units were produced; about 22,000 of them are similar to Mike Salisbury's 1967 cargo truck. The drivetrain was out of the super HD catalog, with a beefy Dana 60 front axle and ultra beefy Dana 70 rear. A Warner Gear T-98A trans and NP-200 divorced transfer case completed the outfit. The engine was an updated version of the 230OHC that had left the civilian lineup in 1965.

CHAPTER 6

1953-1970

A STEADY HAND

THE KAISER-ERA JEEPS

Some historians have called the marriage of Willys-Overland and Kaiser a shotgun wedding. The union of Kaiser-Frazer and Willys-Overland on April 28, 1953, gave Kaiser a much-needed boost. Henry J. Kaiser's car empire was slowly toppling, having lost money since 1948. The successful Kaiser financial empire had been keeping the carmaker afloat and paid $62,000,000 to buy Willys-Overland.

As for Willys-Overland, it wasn't exactly considered one of the "Big-Three," but it was relatively successful in its niche. Many people, the rank and file employees especially, were surprised when to two companies merged. In the long run, it worked out well for Willys. The merger gave the Willys line capital for expansion and growth, and kept the Kaiser side alive for a few more years.

The CJ-3B was an inheritance from Willys-Overland and made its debut the year of the takeover. The early and late CJ-3Bs differed in many ways. If you compare John Hubbard's restified 1954 with Adam Charnock's original 1963 on page 94, you will immediately see the differences in the dash. The CJ-3Bs came in 1957 when the cluster of gauges was changed to a single, integrated unit. They changed from 6- to 12-volt electrical systems at the same time. A dash-mounted T-handle emergency brake replaced the "walking stick" handle in 1961. In the early 1960s, as Kaiser was determined to increase the *Kaiser* name recognition, the stamped "Willys" in the grille, hood, and tailgate was eliminated. The changes in production happened immediately, but it took several years to use up the existing stocks of parts. Tailgates were first, since the 3B shared that piece with the CJ-5. Grilles were next and hoods last. The civilian Bantam trailer is a useful period accessory.

After the merger, Willys-Overland became Willys Motors. Kaiser-Frazer retained its identity, but an umbrella sales organization for both outfits was formed and called Kaiser-Willys. This organization lasted for as long as there were Willys and Kaiser cars, which turned out to be a short period of time. By the mid-1950s, both brands of cars were history. The Jeep side supported the dwindling sales of both brands, and by 1955 the Kaiser car was dead. During the next year, the last of the Willys cars rolled out of the Willow Run, Michigan, plant. Both car brands continued for a time in Brazil, and Kaiser sold the Willow Run plant to GM.

Once lightened of the car burden, the Kaiser-Willys organization found a new focus: utility vehicles. At the time, Willys Motors was the only company solely devoted to that market. The type of vehicle we have come to know as the "sport utility" became increasingly popular starting in the 1950s and 1960s, and Willys Motors was poised to capitalize on the idea. Utility vehicles became an increasing slice of the company's production, alongside commercial and military sales. In the late 1950s and early 1960s, many new ideas were tried and marketed. The quality of vehicle construction improved and sales improved as a result. Things were good for Willys Motors.

In March 1963, Willys Motors changed its name to Kaiser Jeep to give the Kaiser side of the family some market identity. The change came around the same time the Wagoneer was introduced, which was one of Jeep's pivotal moments. This new rig stoked the fires of the smoldering sport utility market and created a new niche: the luxury sport utility. The Wagoneer brought an optional independent front suspension to the four-wheel-drive market, as well as power steering and an automatic transmission. The former item was a first and while the latter items were not firsts (available in Dodge 4x4s from 1957 to 1960), they were close seconds.

By the late 1960s, Kaiser Jeep was relatively healthy, but the line had stagnated in the marketplace and sales were not keeping pace with the growth of trucks and sport utility sales. This was partly due to increased competition. IHC had introduced the Scout in 1961. The Ford Bronco was saddled up in 1966, and the Chevy Blazer fired up in 1969. Jeep wasn't really in bad shape, but it needed a little extra fire in the belly. In 1969, Henry J. Kaiser began serious talks with the ailing American Motors about selling

When the CJ-5 made its debut late in 1954, it was everything the earlier Jeep wasn't and also everything it was. It added more room and comfort to the equation without losing the toughness and adaptability. Note the "Willys" emblem on the side, indicating a preproduction vehicle. Production rigs said "Jeep." The new "All-Weather" top was reputed to be the new age in Jeep tops.

the Jeep division. Jeep accounted for almost half of Kaiser Industries profits, but Henry J. was interested in other investments, such as his growing chemical firms and a new managed health care organization

CJ: KAISER'S INFLUENCE

Kaiser came into the game when the CJ-5's development was well on its way. It made its debut in September 1954, and the CJ-6 followed in 1955. Both rigs were well received and soon became favorites all over the world. The CJ-5 was bigger, more stylish, and more comfortable than the old flatfender. The CJ-5 was given the same treatment as the older CJs by fitting it with all sorts of optional equipment, from air compressors to fire apparatus. There was also a large amount of factory and aftermarket equipment available.

The CJ-6 was a cost-effective addition to the lineup. It was identical in all but a few respects to the CJ-5. The big difference was the longer, 101-inch wheelbase, compared to the 81-inch CJ-5. While the CJ-6 had the same relative payload in pounds, it could carry 50 percent more volume. The CJ-6 was never a big seller, and production never reached more than 20 percent of the CJ-5, and usually ran no more than 10 percent. Even the CJ-3B was built in a larger quantity. It isn't clear why this was the case, since the eternal lament of CJ-5 owners is for more room. Still,

The Kaiser era saw an increase in the commercial applications offered in the Jeep line. This 1956 Civil Defense rescue conversion of a 4x4 Utility Delivery was a cross-country emergency rig.

One of the keys to the success of the Willys Utility line was the 6-226 engine. Purchased from Continental, this 226-ci engine offered 115 horsepower and 190 ft-lbs. in a proven, reliable engine. It finally gave the line a decent power-to-weight ratio.

As the 1950s wore on, the 4x4 Utility Wagon line began to acquire a little pizzazz. This two-tone 1958 was restored by Willys America. *Jane L. Barry/Willy's America*

there were enough sales to keep the line going and the old CJ-6 lasted well into the AMC era.

An interesting fact is that the last flat-fender, the CJ-3B, remained in production alongside the CJ-5 and CJ-6, although it had much lower volumes than before. It continued year after year and finally faded away from the American market in 1968. Looking at the remaining documents, one can see no clear marketing strategy shown for keeping the increasingly retro CJ-3B in the lineup. It appears to be a simple case of a Jeep that was not willing to die, or rather enough buyers around the world wouldn't let it die.

The old 3B continued after its American production ended and was built under license by Hotchkiss of France and VIASA of Spain. Mitsubishi was licensed to produce a variant starting in 1953 and production finally stopped in 1998. Mahindra & Mahindra of India and Willco of Columbia still produce a version of the CJ-3B. This record makes the CJ-3B the most enduring Jeep of all time, with a production run of 47 years and counting.

The Gala or Surrey models (they could never make up their minds what to call them) were sold from 1959 to 1964, excluding 1961. They were used most often by resorts, with some resorts buying 40 units at a time. They came in three color combos: the pink motif of Tropical Rose and Coral Mist; the green motif of Jade Tint Green and Glacier White; and the blue motif of Cerulian Blue and Glacier White. A handful of Pepsi Galas were produced in 1959 for a giveaway in Tulsa, Oklahoma, and featured a yellow color scheme with Pepsi hubcaps.

Only minor changes came to the CJ-5 and CJ-6 model through the 1950s and early 1960s. However, in 1961, buyers were given a new option with the 192-ci Perkins diesel. Offered through the 1969 model year, the British-built oil burner offered 30 miles per gallon economy with performance levels equivalent to the old L-head powered CJs. For grunt, it was unmatched in the lineup until the V6 appeared. With 143 ft-lbs. of torque, it could accomplish a good day's work, albeit slowly.

The addition of an optional V6 was a true innovation when it made its debut for 1966. The 160-horsepower, 225-ci ex-Buick V6 gave the Jeep a wonderful performance boost and a new image, similar to that of the pale,

skinny guy on the beach that shows up the next season with a tan and a bulging chest. For the first time in its life, the CJ had adequate power for road work, if not power to spare. This was a reflection of the growing recreational market, and the RV people did not tolerate a sluggish machine. From then on, almost three-fourths of the CJ-5s produced were ordered with the V6.

Another first for the Kaiser era CJs were the Tuxedo Park models. When introduced in 1961, Tuxedo Park was nothing but an options package that included some chrome goodies, more-comfortable seating, and a special badge. By 1964, the option had grown into the Tuxedo Park Mark IV (the previous Tuxedo Parks had been Mark I, II, and III). The Mark IV was a new, more

cultured animal. It had so many features above and beyond the standard CJ that it received a special designation, CJ-5A (or CJ-6A for the longer rig), and its own parts book addendum. Among the chrome bumpers and bracketry, special wheel covers and colors, it had a column-shift transmission, plush bench seat, improved brakes, and special spring rates to create a soft ride. The Tuxedo Park Mark IV was available through the 1968 model year and could also be ordered with the optional V6 when it made its debut. It was sold in small numbers, averaging out to just under 2,000 vehicles a year over the four years of production.

Kaiser CJs went out with a bang. In 1969, a special options package appeared and the equipped vehicles have been known by package number, 462. The option package added to a V-6 equipped CJ-5 a roll bar, G-70 Goodyear Polyglas tires on 15x8 Kelsey Hayes wheels, limited slip rear differential, chrome bumper and bracketry, oil pressure gauge and ammeter, and a hood stripe on some vehicles. Since the only known pictures of these vehicles were taken at a widely publicized press event for advertising, and no photographs have turned up in the hands of collectors, there is some doubt whether it was ever offered to the general public. The package did, however, provide a springboard for the 1970 Renegade 1 package.

One of the last really exciting ideas from Kaiser Jeep was the CJ-5 Camper option. It was a slide-in unit that hung out the back and had its own set of wheels and suspension to help support the extra load. The camper held four people and could be equipped with all the goodies you would expect from a camper in that era, including a 10,000 BTU heater, propane stove, and gas/electric fridge. The option was produced in 1969 and 1970 but was dropped during the AMC takeover. It was not a big seller but everyone at the time thought it was a great idea.

UTILITY WAGONS AND TRUCKS: RISE AND FALL

The Kaiser merger brought a great many benefits to the wagon and pickup lines. The anemic Willys sixes, the 161-ci L- and F-head units, said goodbye in 1954, and were replaced by the powerful 226-ci engine from Continental. Called the "Red Seal," it was the same reliable unit that powered many Kaiser cars and was a common industrial engine. It brought the wagons into serious contention for a bigger slice of the marketplace and went beyond being strictly commercial. Unfortunately, there were no other major engine upgrades to the line until 1963, when the OHC (Overhead Cam) six made its debut, but that's not to say there wasn't anything interesting going on during that time.

The basic lineup consisted of the Station Wagon (known as the Utility Wagon after 1955), the Panel Delivery (later called Utility Delivery), and the pickup (later known as the Utility Truck). Willys Motors produced several special models, and many were commercial based. Most of the snazzy Station Wagon packages, such as two-tone paint and special trim, occurred with the 4x2 version. Later in the 1950s and 1960s, when the 4x4s were outselling the 4x2s three to one, the four-wheelers were given a more appealing batch of cosmetic options.

The Cargo Personnel Carrier was among the more eye-catching commercial version packages. An open-cab variant of the pickup, it had a slab-sided cargo box reminiscent of the World War II Dodge weapons carrier. It sold in small numbers from 1955 into 1961, with many vehicles being exported. Another interesting commercial adaptation was the Traveller. This conversion took a Delivery body, and added windows and folding, inward-facing rear seats.

The lack of a four-door version of the Station Wagon in the lineup is easily noticeable, and many people have wondered why it wasn't included. In fact, a four-door version was previously available and offered beginning in the early 1950s. The vehicle was converted by Parkway, Willys' contract coachbuilder (it also converted the Panels into Travellers); it's thought that over a hundred four-door Station Wagons were built.

The introduction of the 140-horsepower, 230-ci overhead cam six into the Utility line in May of 1962 was both a breath of fresh air and a death knell. The OHC six was a sprightly beast, and despite some early reliability problems, it gave the slab-sided old Utility some muscles to stretch. The older rigs were 500–800 pounds lighter than the brand new Wagoneer/Gladiator line that also used the new engine. The Utilities were produced in declining numbers alongside the newer Jeep sport-utes and trucks until 1964, when the assembly line was shut down. Many of the Utilities produced during the later years were commercial sales. A large number of Utilities remained unsold after 1964, so they were retitled and sold as 1965s.

The Utilities, which have been affectionately called "an overpowered dumpster with big wheels," carried the company for nearly 30 years. The look, which had grown decidedly antique in the face of the competition, retained a Jeeplike flair that kept sales steady long after market analysts and style experts would have predicted a total demise.

FORWARD CONTROL: GENUINE INNOVATION

A true innovation made its debut in December 1956, and Willys Motors gambled a lot on its success. The Forward Control truck was an innovation both in design and use of company resources. While the cab-over layout made tremendous use of space, under the skin of the two basic models, the 81-inch wheelbase FC-150 (FC for Forward Control) and 103.5-inch wheelbase FC-170 were mechanically derived from two existing platforms, the CJ-5 and the Utility Truck.

Freelance designer Brooks Stevens receives the credit for the FC designs, but he can't be thrown under the bus for the relative failure of the idea in the market. Despite the many advantages, the FCs never caught on. Ford, Dodge, and Chevy all tried similar 4x2 light truck ideas beginning in 1960, but faced the same lukewarm results. Regardless of the public's ho-hum reception, the Jeep FCs gave owners great utility and capacity in a small package.

The FC-150 is reminiscent of a Pekinese dog: short, flat-faced and squat. It could, however, carry the equivalent volume of a standard half-ton pickup. While the driving position was similar to that of a bus, the cab was roomy for two, and visibility was superb. Maneuverability was excellent and

THE TORNADO:
AN ENGINE AHEAD OF ITS TIME

When the overhead cam 230-ci Tornado six made its debut in late 1962, it offered a great deal of power and torque in an economical, moderate displacement engine. Appearing in the J-series Wagoneers and trucks, the Utility line, and a few hundred Forward Controls (1963 only), the Tornado was rated for 140 horsepower and 217 ft-lbs of torque in two-barrel form. It was about equal to the Dodge 225 slant six of the era and a little ahead of the Chevy 235-ci, IHC 240-ci, and Ford 223-ci sixes. The truck six-cylinder wars were still going on in the early 1960s, and the OHC was a strong contender.

Designed by A. C. Sampietro, an engineer who came to the Jeep line from Kaiser, the 230 OHC took many cues from the successful 226-ci L-head Continental six. The lower ends had the same stroke and the engines had identical mounting configurations and interchanged freely. The big changes were on the upper end. Where the L-head design was severely restricted in the breathing department, the OHC was a great inhaler and exhaler, creating a 35 percent increase in power over the 226-ci L-head.

According to Sampietro in a paper written for the Society of Automotive Engineers during the summer of 1962, the official 140-horsepower factory rating for the two-barrel was on the low side. Power and torque graphs in this technical paper show the two-barrel engine producing 155 horsepower at 4,000 rpm and 230 ft-lbs of torque at 2,200 rpm. This put the two-barrel version over Chevy's 261-ci, 150-horsepower inline six and in contention with GMC's gutsy 305-ci, 165-horsepower V6. At the time, IHC, Dodge, and Ford did not have large displacement sixes to put in their lineups. The 140 horsepower figure is more in line with the one-barrel engine's true output. All was not perfect with the OHC, however.

The OHC engine had a couple of weaknesses that soon became apparent. There were oil leaks concentrated around the cam chain cover and engine mounting plate. This problem was cured by sealer and extra fastenings. Another weakness was oil consumption from inadequate valve stem seals and chrome rings. The seals were upgraded in August of 1963, and the chrome rings that took forever to seat were replaced by cast rings in engines built after February 1964. A contributing problem to the engine was the partly blocked oil drainback holes in the head that made the valve stem seal problem worse by retaining more oil in the head.

Even though these problems were largely cured under warranty, the reputation of the engine was tarnished, and it was dropped from the civilian lineup after 1965 and replaced with an OHV pushrod engine from AMC. The 230 was resurrected in a 133-horsepower, one-barrel form for the 1967–1969 military M-715 Gladiator, where it served well. The M-715 engine had a large number of differences from the earlier civilian version. For one, it had a block case with engine mount brackets, so the troublesome front mounting plate was eliminated. Many internal parts were different, and the parts do not always interchange.

Most Jeep fans aren't aware that a four-cylinder version of the OHC engine was developed. It was offered to the Mahindra of India and Brazilian Willys plants for manufacture. It displaced 154 cubic inches and made 102 horsepower and 152 ft-lbs of torque. Apparently, it was not produced anywhere beyond some prototype engines. Many wonder why this powerful little engine didn't make it into the smaller Jeeps as the base four-banger in place of the tired little 72-horsepower F-head.

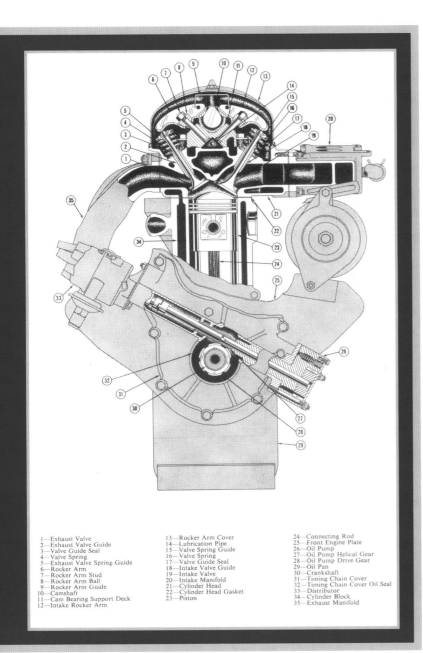

1—Exhaust Valve
2—Exhaust Valve Guide
3—Valve Guide Seal
4—Valve Spring
5—Exhaust Valve Spring Guide
6—Rocker Arm
7—Rocker Arm Stud
8—Rocker Arm Ball
9—Rocker Arm Guide
10—Camshaft
11—Cam Bearing Support Deck
12—Intake Rocker Arm

13—Rocker Arm Cover
14—Lubrication Pipe
15—Valve Spring Guide
16—Valve Spring
17—Valve Guide Seal
18—Intake Valve Guide
19—Intake Valve
20—Intake Manifold
21—Cylinder Head
22—Cylinder Head Gasket
23—Piston

24—Connecting Rod
25—Front Engine Plate
26—Oil Pump
27—Oil Pump Helical Gear
28—Oil Pump Drive Gear
29—Oil Pan
30—Crankshaft
31—Timing Chain Cover
32—Timing Chain Cover Oil Seal
33—Distributor
34—Cylinder Block
35—Exhaust Manifold

the little half-ton could run circles around bigger trucks in tight quarters. Powered by the 134-ci F-head engine, the FC-150 was no speed demon, especially with a full load, but it was economical and reliable.

The early FC-150s were not without problems. They were decidedly nose-heavy when unloaded, causing them to occasionally, when empty, to flip over nose first going down steep hills. The cure was to install a cast-iron weight between the frame rails at the back. The FC-150s built up through July 1958 used the same narrow track, 48.4 inches, as the CJ-5. This made for a tendency for the more top-heavy FC to roll during hard turns. The cure was to use a wider, 57-inch track, and the FC-150 got a stronger Spicer 44F front axle into the bargain as well. FC-150s could be ordered with a standard pickup bed or a flatbed. Willys authorized several utility bodies, and the FC-150s were converted to everything from ice cream trucks to fire engines.

A limited number of a special FC-150 tractor was built to be used with a lightweight fifth wheel trailer setup. The truck was equipped with dual fuel tanks, optional four-speed T-98 transmission, and a fifth wheel towing apparatus. The setup was intended to carry bulk loads rather than heavy loads, but the F-head four must have been hard pressed to move the special trailer, let alone the load. The offering was only semi-official, and it is uncertain just how many tractors were built.

The longer-wheelbase FC-170 trucks were built as one-ton-rated machines, similar to the 4x4 Utility Trucks. They were powered by the 226-ci Super Hurricane six and came standard with a T-90 three-speed, but the burly T-98 Warner Gear four-speed was optional. Like its little brother, the FC-170 offered a great deal of cargo capacity in a more compact size. The 170's bed was a full nine-footer, but the overall length of the truck was 4 inches shorter than a Chevy shortbed (6-foot bed) pickup.

In 1959, Willys Motors offered two high Gross Vehicle Weight (GVW) versions of the FC-170 called the FC-170 DRW. The DRW stood for "dual rear wheels" and these trucks were rated for 8,000- or 9,000-pound GVWs. With a 4,800-pound curb weight, the vehicles had more than 3,000 or 4,000 pounds of cargo capacity. This was accomplished by building the rig on a stout chassis, adding a Spicer 70, dual-wheel rear axle and a Spicer 44FHD front axle. Both units used the same 226-ci engine, and the lower GVW unit had a three-speed transmission while the higher had a HD-four-speed. Most FC-170 DRWs were sold with flatbeds or as a cab and chassis for conversion.

Like the FC-150, the FC-170 chassis was used a great deal in commercial conversions. The DRW models were popular as fire truck conversions. According to factory production records from 1963, 685 FC-170s were fitted with 230 OHC sixes. Another 17 were mounted with the three-cylinder, 170-ci Cerlist diesel commonly used in the M-series military line. Little documentation exists on either engine installation, but both appear to be well-reasoned adaptations. Coming in the twilight of the FC's life, the FC-170s were the engineers' and marketing department's last hope of breathing new life into the line.

The FC line soldiered on until 1964 when production stopped. At the beginning of 1965, the remaining units were retitled and sold as 1965s. The FC was one of Willys Motors true conceptual triumphs, but like so many good

This is the newest old Jeep you have ever seen. Adam Charnock's two-owner 1963 CJ-3B has less than 5,500 original miles and still mounts the original tires and top. It is still running on its original spark plugs and wearing the original Tree Bark Brown metallic paint. Charnock's Jeep was ordered with a heater, Goodyear 7.00-15 Suburbanite tires, drawbar and trailer hitch, a full top (by White Manufacturing), and "Power-Lock" locking hubs. It was apparently never fitted with a back seat.

When the FC-150 Forward Control was introduced in December 1956, it broke new ground on many fronts. It was the first light-duty forward control offered in America as well as the first light-duty 4x4 forward control. The early FC-150, like collector and FC expert Craig Brockhaus' super original 1957, used a narrow 48.4 inch track (the same as the CJs). Craig's low-mileage rig still wears its original All-Service tires and Jeep-approved Ramsey winch kit. It was also fitted with a dual rear wheel conversion for stability by the original owner.

automotive ideas that have failed in the market, timing was the key element. In this case, it worked against them.

WAGONEER: TRUE SPORT UTE

The Wagoneer broke new ground when it was introduced in November 1962. The Wagoneer bridged the gap between the civilized car and the 4x4 truck better than any other company's previous attempt. It combined elements of both vehicles into a category that has lately been called a Sports Utility Vehicle (SUV).

In its top-of-the-line Custom trim, the Wagoneer was as comfortable and well appointed as many mid-priced cars of the era, but it had one advantage.

The Wagoneer could carry a heavier load than any station wagon, easily tow heavier loads, and it had four-wheel drive to deal with bad roads and weather. It was not built as a die-hard four-wheeler, although the stripped-down Wagoneers with go-to-work options packages were no slouches in that department.

The Wagoneers brought a few innovations to the market. One was the OHC six, which, despite its small 230-ci displacement, was quite peppy. Another innovation was the optional independent front suspension (IFS), a first in the SUV market. Some have claimed that the Wagoneer was also first in offering an automatic transmission, but the 1957–1960 Dodge trucks, including the Town Wagon, had automatic available. Still, the Wagoneer stood alone in offering the 4x4 option when it made its debut.

The Wagoneers came as two- or four-door station wagons, or as a two-door Panel Delivery. The two-door station wagon versions accounted for less than 10 percent of sales and were dropped after 1968. The Panel was sold in similarly small numbers and was dropped the same year. Small numbers of 4x2 Wagoneers and Panel Deliveries were also built into 1968.

Evolution came quickly for the Wagoneer. For 1965, a V8 engine was offered in the form of the 327-ci, 250-horsepower American Motors V8, and it was backed up by the bulletproof GM TH-400 automatic. The IFS option was dropped late in 1965, as was the OHC six. The OHC six was

The long-wheelbase FC-170 pickup made its debut on a 103.5-inch wheelbase and was rated for a one-ton capacity. Unlike the FC-150, which only came with a four-cylinder, the larger rig had the 6-226 engine.

The single rear FC-170s were often fitted with specialty beds. Jim and Peg Marski's 1959 FC-170 has a factory stake bed and hydraulic lift gate.

Partway through 1958, the FC-150 received a stabilizing influence in the form of a wider track. It jumped to 57 inches, (the same size as the FC-170) and had a stronger Dana 44 front axle. Don Haynes' 1959 shows off the filled-out look of the wider track. The deluxe cab, with extra side windows, was bright and spacious enough for two occupants. An engine box seat was available for extra passengers. The engine on an FC is not particularly accessible for major repairs, but oil changes and tune-ups are a snap.

One of the highlights of the FC's production was the introduction of the FC-170 DRW (Dual Rear Wheel) model in 1959. It arrived in 8,000 and 9,000 GVW and could be fitted with a variety of specialty beds. The stakebed was common, but the FC found a big market with fire truck conversion companies.

replaced by the 232-ci six, another AMC engine. By 1968, the 327, which was being phased out by AMC, was replaced with the more powerful 350-ci Buick power plant that, ironically, was similar to the 225-ci Buick V6 that was being used in the CJs.

The biggest news in 1965 was the introduction of a 1966 model that would create another first for Jeep in the four-wheel-drive market, the Super Wagoneer. This vehicle literally created the luxury SUV market. The limited edition "dirt-limo" was powered by a pumped up, 270-horsepower four-barrel version of the AMC 327-ci coupled with a TH-400 automatic with a special console shifter and single-speed transfer case.

The Super Wagoneer's exterior featured a padded vinyl top and roof rack, as well as special colors, gold accent side strips, 8.45-15 tires, and snazzy wheel covers. Inside, the driver was cosseted by plush, contoured bucket seats, padded high-grade vinyl panels, plush carpets, a four-speaker AM-FM with eight-track tape player, and air conditioning. Power steering and brakes were standard, as well as a power-operated tailgate and tinted glass.

There were 3,989 Super Wagoneers built from late 1965 to mid-1969. They truly set the stage for the luxury SUV market. Land Rover likes to think its 1970 Range Rover set the plush 4x4 standard, but it wasn't until 1981 that the Range Rover even rivaled the Super Wagoneer for features.

The "Swedish Bus" was a conversion of the FC-170 built in Sweden. Jeep liked it so much that they brought it over for study in the early 1960s.

GLADIATOR TRUCKS: STYLISH STALWARTS

When the 1963 line of Jeep trucks rolled out, Kaiser Jeep had placed a great deal of faith in the vehicles. Kaiser Jeep pickups rivaled the "Big-Three" for features and options, especially with the 4x4 models. The Jeep trucks brought some of the same innovations to the 4x4 world as did the Wagoneer, namely the OHC six and the IFS option. The truck IFS option was available for the half-ton trucks, but it differed in that it featured a stronger Model 44IFS front differential instead of the Wagoneer Model 27IFS.

By the early 1960s, the Utility Wagon models had reverted to two general trim styles. The 4x2s used the "missile" motif and the 4x4s had a chrome strip that turned down on the cowl, just aft of the fender. There were, of course, basic models of a single color.

Most of the 1966-and-up CJs were powered by the optional V6. By 1969, the CJ-5 divided windshield disappeared, as well as the vestigial battery box cover that the CJ inherited from the M-38A1. This CJ is fitted out with the optional Goodyear Suburbanite tires and a white top from (no pun intended) White manufacturing. The side step was optional.

The basic CJ-6 was ready to work, but this one has the 225-ci V6 added. It is running the standard 6.00-16 All-Service nondirectional tires. These are the standard seats, but in this era the passenger seat was a $75.80 option. The V6, incidentally, cost $215.30.

Top: Tuxedo Park is a name that's nearly forgotten these days, but from 1964 to 1968 Tuxedo Park Mark IV (CJ-5A or CJ-6A) was an extra plush version of the CJ. The Marski Jeep Collection has two Tuxedo Park Mark IVs, this one being of the CJ-6A variety. Note the chrome front bumper and chrome bracketry. In addition, they used a comfortable bench seat, column shift, bigger brakes, and soft-ride springs.

Left: One of the most interesting offerings from the end of the Kaiser era was the Camper. A Jeep CJ with the V6 option and 4.88 gears was recommended, and a drawbar was required. The halfcab, shown here, was another necessary item unless you went topless. The basic camper was available through 1969 and into 1970, and was a $2,198 option.

The king of the Jeep sport utility vehicles was the Wagoneer. Rolling out late in 1962 as a 1963 model, it combined the attributes of a four-wheel-drive truck with a station wagon. Interior appointments rivaled the average station wagon of the day. To 1968, Wagoneers were available with two or four doors. The Marski's two-door is optioned up with the Borg-Warner automatic, power steering and brakes, as well as a compass.

The J-trucks had a complicated classification system. From 1963 to 1965, they used the J-200 and J-300 terms, and the Wagoneer was known as the J-100. From mid-1965 on, the trucks became the J-2000 and J-3000 series. The differences in the J-200/2000 and J-300/3000 were that the former were based on a 120-inch wheelbase and the latter on a 126-inch wheelbase. A J-4000 made its debut in 1970 and had a 132-inch wheelbase. Within these categories, the trucks were divided up by bed type (Thriftside or Styleside) and GVW. There were a multitude of possible combinations and the sales literature was, and is, thoroughly confusing.

Like the Wagoneer, the J-trucks received the V8 in 1965 and lost the OHC Tornado in exchange for the AMC 232-ci. The trucks also gained the Buick 350 for 1968. One early change the trucks didn't get was the Wagoneer grille change in 1965. The Wagoneers had a full width "toothy smile," and the trucks kept their "beaver teeth" front end until 1970. Overall, the J-truck line didn't receive much attention through the Kaiser era unless it dovetailed with the Wagoneer.

JEEPSTER COMMANDO: A BETTER JEEP SPORTS CAR

While the Jeepster concept was way ahead of its time in 1948, the 1967–1971 reprisal of the idea for the Jeepster Commando (C-101 Models) was right on time. Function and flair combined with spirited performance made this rig a *true* sport utility vehicle. The basic model was powered by the old F-head four, but few were purchased that way. Most buyers ordered the Commando with the optional 225-ci V6, the same unit that was used in the CJ. The V6 was optionally backed by the GM TH-400, which was about three times stronger than what was needed for the engine and vehicle combination.

Initially there were five possible versions of the Jeepster Commando on two basic platforms. The 8701 Convertible, complete with two-tone paint, Continental kit and rear deck, an optional power top and upscale trimmings, was the flagship. The remaining models were all based on the 8705 roadster. When equipped with a full-length hardtop, an "F" was added to the

In 1965, the Wagoneer exchanged its "buck-toothed beaver" look for a wide chrome smile. The new grille made its debut that year and variations of this grille lasted to 1979. This was also the first year for the 327-ci V8, an AMC transplant, with the six as a base engine. By mid-year, the 230 OHC was gone, replaced by the 232-ci six, another AMC engine.

designation. When equipped with a bulkhead and half cab, the vehicle became a pickup with an "H" designation. Roadsters with no top had an "O" to fill up the hole in the VIN. The snap-on softtop was an option on the roadster. Except for the true convertible, the tops were all removable and interchangeable.

Beyond the deletion of the full-boat convertible and substitution of the model 8702 "Austere Convertible" in 1968, there were no major changes in the Jeepster Commando line. Some of the few changes occurred during the AMC era in the form of special models, but they will be covered here because AMC completely revamped the Commando for 1972. The New Commando is covered in the AMC chapter.

The SC-1 model appeared in 1971 as a 1971 1/2 model. It wore a Butterscotch Gold paint job with a woodgrain stripe and had SC-1 identification. The base unit was an optioned-out station wagon model with a luggage rack.

The most rare C-101 variant is the Hurst Jeepster. This was one of AMC's first attempts at lighting a fire under the Jeepster Commando lineup. Conceived in 1970, the Hurst-Jeep collaboration took a high option V6 station wagon in white, added some racing stripes, a nonfunctional hood scoop that mounted a functional

tach, special Hurst shifter, and G-70-15 Goodyear tires on 6-inch rims. It was topped off with special badging inside and out. Some 500 units, automatic and manual, were projected for production, but fewer than 100 were sold in 1971 and they were all automatics.

TWO-WHEELERS: SLOW SELLERS

All through the Kaiser era, two-wheel-drive versions of most Jeep products were available. With only a few exceptions, they were not sold in significant numbers. One of the exceptions was the certain Post Office vehicles that were built in the commercial plant in South Bend, Indiana, that eventually became the AM General factory. When purchasing Jeep trucks, in most cases, you could buy a vehicle in two- or four-wheel drive. In the 1950s, especially on the Station Wagon side, some of the most option-laden Jeeps were two-wheelers. The Utility Trucks had been divested of the 4x2 option back in 1951, except for some commercial special orders. From the beginning of the Kaiser era to the late 1950s, the 4x2 lines had the most appealing visual and comfort options. Two- and three-tone paint, special trim, and fancy wheel covers were the order of the day. The trim and paint schemes of the 4x4s and 4x2s were kept distinctly different, with the off-roaders being more austere.

The first luxury sport utility vehicle was built by Jeep in the form of the 1966–1969 Super Wagoneer. With a high-zoot set of options, it was the most expensive Jeep built to that time: a whopping $5,943. In 1965 (1966 model year), it was $2,200 more expensive than the Custom Wagoneer.

One particularly interesting 4x2-only package was the Maverick. It appeared in late 1958 while Willys Motors was a sponsor of the *Maverick* television show, starring James Garner. It had a special chrome trim, tartan pattern vinyl upholstery, and other goodies, in addition to a special serial number. Even though the show was cancelled in 1960, the package lasted until 1964.

In 1956, a tiny two-wheeler made its debut in the form of the DJ-3A Dispatcher. It was based on the CJ-3A and resurrected the low-hood, flat fender body, as well as the L-head engine. The basic DJ could be outfitted in a large number of ways, as a hardtop or in several softtop varieties. Not many DJs were purchased as basic transportation, but they saw much use as resort vehicles, light commercial rigs, and the first of many Postal Jeeps.

The DJ-3A topic can't be left behind without talking about the Gala, later called the Gala Surrey. So many DJ-3As had been purchased for use in resorts that a special Gala model was introduced for 1958. The package changed over the 1958–1964 sales period, but the pink units with pink and white striped seats are the best known.

When the DJ-3A was retired in 1965, a similar unit, the DJ-5, was offered based on the CJ-5 line. Both the a DJ-5 and a DJ-6 units were offered from 1965 and lasted until 1973, when production was handed off to AM General. Similar to the earlier DJs, the DJ-5 and DJ-6 models came in a variety of styles and even could be ordered with the V6.

Rounding up the 4x2 section is the FJ. The FJ was a compact van based on the CJ chassis. The FJ could stand for "Forgotten Jeep" because so few people remember them. The FJ-3 and FJ-3A were introduced in 1960 and lasted until 1964. The FJ-3 was a special Post Office version and the 3A was the commercial version. They differed in steering wheel location (the FJ-3's steering was on the right-hand side), body length, and transmission type (the PO version often had an automatic). After 1964, the FJ-6 van, based on the DJ-6 chassis, made its debut and lasted into the 1970s, but by that time, AM General was producing the vehicles.

The Marski's 1968 Super Wagoneer has been modified cosmetically with the addition of alloy wheels, although they mimic the original hubcaps. Reputedly, this Super Wagoneer once belonged to comedian Buddy Hackett.

A Gladiator truck could be outfitted in a multitude of ways, including with the stakebed on this 1963. When the trucks made their debut, they did so with a staggering variety of options.

In 1965, the Gladiators with the Townside bed were stylish in a Jeeplike way. This 4x4 has a 327 V8 and Goodyear Hi-Miler Extra-Grip tires.

The model 8701 Jeepster Commando was the top of the line for the short time it was produced. It was a true convertible with a manual or power-operated top. The two-tone paint and the Continental kit are what set this model apart from the rest. Most 8701s were built for the 1967 model year, with a few built in 1968 and 1969.

In the Jeepster Commando line, the 8705F Station Wagon was the best seller. This 1970 model has the optional V6 ($210), Suburbanite tires ($81.72), Trim package B (roof rack, wheel covers, chrome bumpers and trim for $349.72), and automatic transmission ($325.60). The grand total of the options adds up to $4,174.04.

Less popular, but useful in a "Gentleman Farmer" way, was the 8705H Jeepster Commando pickup. It could haul a 750-pound payload with the standard springs. With the exception of the Suburbanite tires and V6, this one is a standard version.

RISE AND FALL

THE AMC ERA JEEPS

The AMC era was a roller-coaster ride for Jeep. Never did it hit higher highs or lower lows than it did from 1970 to 1987. It's unlikely that the Jeep name would have ever been allowed to die, but it came closer to that than ever before under American Motors. On the other hand, AMC gave Jeep a new look and moved it out of the increasingly stodgy Kaiser stable. The AMC era was a tumultuous and interesting period.

American Motors Corporation (AMC) was formed in 1954 and combined the Nash and Hudson companies. The cars remained under the Nash and Hudson nameplates until 1958, when they were combined to create a new car line under the Rambler badge. In 1968, the model line was rebadged American Motors. In 1970, AMC purchased Jeep for $10 million and 5.5 million shares of stock in AMC. Although AMC had to stretch for resources to make the deal, it gave the ailing Kaiser Jeep some fresh blood and a new market to pursue.

The first hints of a future Jeep/AMC connection came back in 1960. At that time, AMC was in the midst of building the Mighty Mite. George Romney, then president of AMC, was excited at the prospect of military contracts and wanted to go looking for more. Roy Chapin, then a vice president, proposed buying Willys Motors and, according to some reports, set up a meeting with Henry J. Kaiser to work out a deal. In the end, Romney decided against the purchase, but Chapin didn't forget the idea.

The Wrangler YJ made its debut in May 1986 and went into production for 1987 just in time for the purchase by Chrysler. This Wrangler Laredo from 1987 represents the top of the line in the initial introduction.

nother connection to tie Kaiser Jeep and AMC together came in the mid-1960s while Kaiser Jeep and AMC were doing some engine business. In 1964, they negotiated a deal to sell the Rambler 327-ci V8 and the 232-ci inline OHV sixes for use in the 1965 Wagoneers and Gladiators, to replace the OHC 230 six. Chapin again brought up the AMC/Jeep idea, but the new president, Roy Abernathy, nixed the idea as financially unfeasible.

By 1967, Roy Chapin had climbed to the top of the AMC ladder but at a terrible time for the company. AMC was hanging by a thread for a couple of years, but as Chapin steered the company off the rocks, he had time to entertain the AMC-Jeep merger and talked to Henry J. By late 1969, a deal had been worked out and in February 1970, Kaiser Jeep became AMC Jeep and a new era began.

CHANGES OF FOCUS

One of the first changes engineered for the new era was a more youthful, fun, and sporty image for the Jeep. AMC didn't have much time for changes in 1970, but it started on the next year's models with a vengeance. A great deal of excitement about new opportunities for market share and sales was generated, but staggering financial losses left many stockholders regretting the purchase of Jeep. Engineering changes, restructuring, and integrating the Jeep and AMC dealer networks also took a great deal of time, and some of the necessary changes were painful.

A huge change came in 1971, when the commercial side of the former Kaiser Jeep, last referred to as the General Products Division, was spun off into a wholly owned subsidiary called AM General. This separated all the commercial and military efforts from the purely civilian markets. Gradually the Jeep and AM General sales began to tick upwards for 1971 and with $10 million net earnings reported that year, it appeared that the transition crisis was over

By 1972, all Jeep model lines had undergone major changes, and the dealer and distribution network had been thoroughly overhauled. The Kaiser influence was largely gone, and AMC Jeep began to feel the positive effects coming from the burgeoning SUV market and its growing dominance. One of AMC's foremost goals was to incorporate as much existing AMC engineering into the Jeep lineup as possible, including engines, axles, and small parts. By 1972, this was largely done and the results were good, especially in the engine departments.

Throughout the 1970s, AMC actually started to rock and roll. Sales of Jeeps and AMC cars were good, but many of Jeep's export operations had suffered since the Kaiser days. In 1979, AMC reached an agreement with Renault of France to distribute Renault cars in North America. In the midst of the fuel crisis, a line of very fuel-efficient cars was a good thing to sell. In exchange, Renault gained the right to distribute Jeeps in France.

The early 1980s brought a recession and the good times and quality control quickly slipped away from AMC. In the rush for the gold, AMC Jeep had let product quality slip to dangerously low levels and, with the recession, it was beginning to take a serious bite out of sales. AMC soon learned just how dependent it was on the profitable Jeep line. As sales slipped lower, the

financial pain became acute. Jeep sales had dropped a whopping 51 percent from 1971 to 1980.

Renault began to invest more money into AMC and owned 46 percent of the company by the end of 1980, but the losses mounted. Selling off AM General in 1983 helped relieve some stress, but what really helped was the introduction of the XJ Cherokee line. A percentage of the recent losses had been the cost involved with bringing this new vehicle to market. It was a gamble, but one that paid off. The XJ was a major success, but there were great debts to pay and much to catch up on.

In 1973 and again in 1976, the Super Jeep package offered a low-cost, eye-catching color scheme that could be ordered on a relatively standard CJ-5.

Even with the successes, there was a downside. Elements inside Renault had long advocated dumping AMC on the first unsuspecting buyer. George Besse, the chairman of Renault, had stood in the way, but shortly after his apparently unrelated murder in Paris late in 1986, Renault entered into a deal with Chrysler Corporation to sell the whole AMC Corporation.

CJ: AMC UPGRADES THE WORKHORSE

The 1970 and 1971 CJs saw few real changes beyond the Kaiser influence. Most of the changes involved cosmetics and the options package. In late 1970, a sporty model of the CJ-5 was introduced and called the Renegade I. It isn't clear whether the Renegade was Kaiser's last gasp or AMC's first shot. Either way, the CJ received a healthy dose of sportiness.

The 1972 model year brought major changes to the CJ lineup; there were three engine options, all AMC transplants. The engine changes necessitated an increase in wheelbase of three inches for all models. The CJ-5

The Golden Eagle package first appeared on 1977 CJ-5s and CJ-7s and lasted to 1980. It could be ordered with any available drivetrain package. A Golden Eagle package, with its lurid eagle hood decal, was also seen on the J-10 truck and with a SJ Cherokee package.

In 1982, the world famous Jeepers Jamboree celebrated its 30th anniversary. Jeep designed a CJ-7 to commemorate the milestone. Limited to 2,500 individually numbered copies, the Jamboree Edition came with a framed certificate of authenticity. The package included a wide variety of goodies, although the winch and brush guard were optional and installed at the dealer.

The top Scrambler was the SL Sport, and the Marski Collection's 1984 is an optioned out version with wood siderails, a 20-gallon fuel tank, side steps, and a dealer-installed Ramsey winch.

stretched to 84 inches and the CJ-6 to 104 inches. The 1972 and newer CJs are commonly called "Long Nose" CJs and the earlier units "Short Nose," because the extra length was added in front of the cowl.

The standard 232-ci six had as much grunt as the optional V6 in the Kaiser days. The old F-head four was finally dropped after 22 years in service. The other engine option was the 258-ci six that was 10 percent more powerful than the baseline power plant. The last option—and hang onto your hat, Mabel—was the 304-ci V8 engine. This was the first and last V8 offered in a CJ. The transmission and transfer case choices changed due to the

engine swaps and the axles were upgraded. The front Dana 30 axle incorporated the new open knuckle design, and the rear featured the new flanged-axle Dana 44.

In 1973, the Super Jeep, another special CJ-5, appeared. With wild paint and decal color schemes, Super Jeeps were real eye catchers. The vehicle was positioned to offer the same type of whiz-bang appearance and presence of the Renegade without the high cost. The Special Production Order (SPO) Renegade package could be ordered as a similarly functional package. The Super Jeep reappeared in 1976 and 1977.

Introduced as a 1981 1/2 model, the CJ-8 Scrambler combined the attributes of a CJ with those of a small pickup. Sales were marginal and second guessers fault AMC Jeep's ineffective marketing of the useful machine. Small pickups were hot at that time and the Scrambler should have been marketed that way. This 1983 SR Sport in Chestnut Brown also has chrome steel wheels that were a part of the SL package. It would normally have come with white-spoked steel wheels. In this era, only the 2.5-liter four or the 258-ci six were available.

The Wagoneer generally fared well with the AMC buyout. It regularly evolved and was actively marketed. This 1972 had some minor trim changes from the Kaiser era units but the powertrain had been largely changed to AMC components. It wasn't until 1975 that the Wagoneer line acquired its signature woodgrain side panels.

In 1979, the Wagoneer was offered in two versions; the Wagoneer Limited with the full woodgrain treatment, and the standard Wagoneer. This standard Wagoneer has the optional two-tone paint, American Racing alloy wheels, and bucket seats.

Earth-shattering news came in 1976, when the CJ-7 was introduced. Developed in 1972 under the project name CJ-5.5, the CJ-7 was a CJ-5 stretched 10.4 inches in the middle. This allowed the CJ to carry hard doors with rollup windows for the first time. The CJ-7 also introduced an automatic transmission and full-time four-wheel drive into the package. More options were later added, including disc brakes, air conditioning, and a host of other comforts and conveniences. The CJ-7 proved to be the most popular CJ of all time, with nearly 380,000 sold over a 10-year production run. That's equal to two-thirds of the *entire* CJ-5 run.

What AMC Jeep giveth, it also taketh away. When the CJ-7 was introduced, the slow-selling CJ-6 went goodbye in the domestic market for 1976. It soldiered on as an export until 1981. The V8 disappeared in California in 1979 due to emissions concerns, and was no longer available in the rest of the country by 1981. In a 1983 maelstrom of bad press, the CJ-5 was discontinued. The street antics of a trail-capable, short-wheelbase vehicle were no longer regarded as safe for the public.

AMC introduced a large number of special packages to the CJ line besides the Renegade. These include the 1977–1980 Golden Eagle, the 1980 1/2 Golden Hawk, the 1982 Jamboree Edition that was limited to 2,500 copies and celebrated the 30th anniversary of the Jeepers Jamboree,

the 1980–1986 Laredo, the street oriented 1982–1983 Limited and the 1979 Silver Anniversary CJ-5.

In 1975, AMC Jeep brought out a package that was one of the most enduring and popular of all, the Levi's interior. Levi's and Jeep capitalized on the popularity of Levi's denim jeans by providing denimlike upholstery. The early version came complete with a Levi's decal in the fender, but later the package was listed as the Denim option.

Introduced as an 1981 1/2 model, a new CJ provided more room and a new concept. The CJ-8, more commonly called the Scrambler, was a 103.5-inch wheelbase rig similar in concept to the CJ-6, but with more pickuplike qualities. With a removable bulkhead, the CJ-8 could be used as an open- or closed-top pickup, or a full-length top could be fitted to make it into a walk-through station wagon. Despite the obvious appeal, the CJ-8 never was a major success, with only around 30,000 units built. Three to five percent the vehicles built were export models. The CJ-8 was discontinued after 1985. Today, the Scrambler is one of the hottest Jeeps out there. Go figure!

A very rare CJ is the CJ-10. Introduced in 1982, this export-only 3/4 ton truck was based on the CJ style. It was part of the AM General sale in 1983, so it was actually under AMC control for a short time. The CJ-10 came on a 119-inch wheelbase and consisted of a CJ body shortened to a half cab. The

After the 1984 introduction of the XJ-based Wagoneer, the big-jeep SJ-based version was called the Grand Wagoneer. Options were frozen at an upscale level. Changes were few and not readily visible, but this is the Wagoneer most of us picture in our minds. This 1985 model was built just a couple of years before the Chrysler takeover.

front end was restyled and the rectangular headlights were placed in the fenders. The CJ-10 was powered by either a non-emissions 151-ci four, a non-emissions 258-ci six, or a Nissan six-cylinder diesel. A variant was the CJ-10A, which was a short-wheelbase 4x2 version used as a military aircraft tug and was built by AM General. The CJ-10 was discontinued after 1985.

In 1986, the CJ line finally disappeared for good. Continuous bad press from safety advocates finally pushed AMC into discontinuing the line. It was replaced in 1987 with the Wrangler, codenamed the YJ, which was a cleverly disguised CJ with a few well-chosen mechanical changes. A lower stance, improved suspension, and wider axles made the YJ more stable and safe on

the street. The adaptation might have happened anyway, but AMC needed to expunge the CJ name from the lineup to improve the corporate image.

WAGONEER: POPULAR AND PROFITABLE

The Wagoneer fared very well under the AMC banner. By January 1971, AMC engines had been fitted to all the Wagoneers. This was an easy adaptation, since the six was already being used by Kaiser, and all the AMC engines use the same bellhousing pattern. The 258 became the base engine, with the 304 and 360-ci engines as options. One exception was the low-volume 1971 Super Custom model 1414X. It was a full-boat luxury

In 1974, the two-door SJ returned as the Cherokee. It offered a low-cost base model alternative to the Wagoneer and perhaps a sportier look. This 1975 Cherokee "S" was the upscale version of the two-door Cherokee.

Wagoneer, similar to the Super Wagoneer, with special trim and a sunroof, and it was powered by the Buick 350-ci.

The full-time four-wheel-drive Quadra-Trac system was added in 1973 and made the application of four-wheel drive very user friendly. A full-time system became standard fare for most Wagoneers through the AMC and Chrysler eras. The early Quadra-Trac transfer case (a Model BW-1339 from Borg Warner) was paired with the GM TH-400 automatic until 1979.

Many changes were made involving engine choices for the Wagoneer throughout the AMC era. In 1973, the 304 was dropped and replaced with the two-barrel 360. A four-barrel 360-ci took over top dog duties. In 1974, the 258 six was dropped and the 360 two-barrel took over as the baseline engine, the 360 four-barrel took over middle duties, and a 401-ci thumper took over as top dog. This lineup remained until 1978, but the next year the only engine available was a 360 two-barrel. By 1981, the 258 returned as the only available California engine, and a severely choked 360 two-barrel became the top dog elsewhere in America. This remained the status quo until the 1987 Chrysler takeover.

For 1977, a four-door Cherokee "S" was introduced as a less expensive alternative to the Wagoneer. In reality, the Cherokee "S" was as well appointed as the Wagoneer. This 1979 shows off the optional two-tone Russet Metallic/Olympic White colors. The alloy wheels were part of the "S" package. Take note of the new grille and rectangular headlights that made their debut for 1979.

N-8-74-68-2

By 1975, the truck lines had undergone some styling changes along with the new engines. This 1975 J-20 4x4 has a Custom Cab, two-tone paint, and alloy wheels. This J-20 has the 131-inch wheelbase.

A number of model changes came to the Wagoneer. Through 1974, the Standard and Custom trim Wagoneers were still available. When the lower level Cherokee was introduced in 1974, the only available Wagoneer trim was equivalent to a Custom. In 1978, a new Limited Wagoneer was added to the lineup. It was truly a top-of-the-line package with just about everything considered luxurious or convenient as standard.

In 1979 a bold new grille and front-end treatment made its debut on all models. Another new variation appeared for 1981 in the form of the Brougham package. It was positioned as a middle level offering between the standard Wagoneer and the Limited. This remained in the lineup up through 1983. In 1984, the midsized Cherokee XJ model made its debut and upset the SJ applecart. The upscale version of the XJ was called the Wagoneer. The older, larger unit was named Grand Wagoneer, and the options packages were severely limited, but remained upscale. AMC fully expected the old Grand Wagoneer to fade away but the company learned that the big Jeep was still popular, despite 22-year-old styling and fuel economy that would make an Arab oil sheik smile.

The later version of the Honcho used updated graphics. Shown here is a 1979 model with new grille and front end.

JEEP COMMANDO: UPGRADED TO OBLIVION

AMC made few changes to the C-101 Jeepster Commando until the 1972 model year. That year, the "Jeepster" part of the name was dropped and the unit was fitted with AMC engines. Similar to the CJs, the swap required a 3-inch wheelbase stretch, and the Commando wheelbase grew to 104 inches. The new engine lineup matched the CJ: the 232-ci six as a base, with the 258-ci six and 304-ci V8 as middle and upper level options.

The stretch job gave AMC the chance for a styling exercise, and the company took full advantage of it. A large egg-crate grille replaced the more Jeeplike grille.

Serious Jeep fans were fond of making ribald comments on the new look, but sales did not seem to drop off. The great new powertrain choices probably had something to do with it. The rest of the vehicle remained the same, although the convertible was dropped from the lineup, leaving just the roadster, pickup, and station wagon.

Midway through 1972, an SC-2 model made its debut that was similar to the 1971 SC-1: It had the similar Butterscotch paint and wood trim. For 1973, the model designation changed to C-104, but few other changes were made. In July 1973, the last Commando was built and the line shut down for good. That ended a six-year run for a vehicle that picked up where the old 1948–1951 Jeepster had left off. The C-101 and C-104 were about as close to a true Jeep sports cars as the company had ever been.

JEEP TRUCKS: A CASE OF NEGLECT

Jeep trucks converted to the AMC engines just as fast as the Wagoneers. One of AMC's first jobs with the trucks was to reduce the staggering 29-choice array of wheelbase and weight rating combinations down to 13. Wheelbases were reduced to two, 120 inches and 132 inches, and the

The late 1970s were near the end of the snazzy era for the Jeep truck. This 1979 J-20 has the Custom package and the optional brush guard.

At the end of the Jeep truck era, the pickup line had received only a few upgrades. The forward-facing lip on the roof had been smoothed and a rather attractive grille emerged in 1981. As the 1980s progressed, trim and options decreased. This 1987 was the last of the line, though there were a few 1988 preproduction units built before Chrysler pulled the plug.

The Commando was AMC's variation on the Jeepster theme. Some Jeep fans debated the look, but the line of powerplants really added to the driving aspect. This new Commando could be ordered with a V8.

model designations were J-2000 and J-4000. The name "Gladiator" was also dropped by 1972. The number of paint and trim options increased. The Thriftside and Townside style cargo bodies were retained, engine choices were the same as the Wagoneer, and trim levels remained as Standard and Custom.

Similar to the Wagoneer, the lower GVW trucks of 1973 had the Quadra-Trac full-time four-wheel-drive option available with the 360-ci V8. More changes of designations and powertrain came in 1974. Underneath, a new, open-knuckle Dana 44 front axle appeared along with an option for the 401-ci four-barrel engine. These changes necessitated a change in wheelbase, and the two basic truck types sat on new 119- and 131-inch wheelbases. The designation changed to J-10 for the shorter rigs and J-20 for the longer. Several GVW ratings were offered with each type.

Two trim packages were offered in 1974, the Custom and the Pioneer: the former being the old standard trim, the latter the high-zoot option. Through the next few years, the Pioneer package went farther upscale in response to general industry trend and acquired a woodgrain stripe à la the Wagoneer.

In 1977, the Honcho, an all-new package, appeared and injected some serious pizzazz into the truck line. With the wide track axles, big tires, spoker-type wheels, tastefully dazzling colors and striping, and the new optional Sportside bed with a sport bar (nonfunctional roll bar), the truck was a knockout. It gave the old lines of the truck new definition. Best of all it could be outfitted with the 401-ci engine for as much go as show. The Honcho package was popular and lasted until 1983. Other specials that came to the truck lines over the years included the 1980–1983 Laredo,

If you look at it from a non-Jeep point of view, the 1972–1973 Commando's egg-crate grille is rather attractive. The Commando line was dropped after 1973. Sales were on par with previous years right to the end, so either that wasn't enough for AMC management or there were other reasons not so apparent.

the 1978–1980 Golden Eagle, the 1978–1979 10-4 and the 1977–1981 Snow Boss.

The 1970s were the heyday of the AMC Jeep truck. By the early 1980s, AMC was spending less time on the aging truck line. If it received anything, it was only because there were carryover parts from upgrades to the Grand Wagoneer. Following production figures, there is a definite decline starting in 1983, but whether the neglect begat the sales drop or the sales drop begat the neglect is not certain. The Jeep pickups lasted into the 1987 model year. AMC actually published 1988 sales info, but after the Chrysler takeover, the Jeep truck line was mercifully euthanized.

CHEROKEE SJ: THE PEOPLE'S WAGONEER

The SJ Cherokee line made its debut in 1974 as a variation of the big Jeep theme and a lower cost alternative to the increasingly full-boat Wagoneer. The first time the term "sport utility" appeared in Jeep literature was in an ad for the Cherokee. Initially, Cherokees were two-doors and it had been six years since two-door big Jeeps were offered. They were heavily restyled versions of the old Wagoneer two-door, with big side windows. The Cherokee "S" model was the mid-level package to which lots of options could be added.

A variation on the variation was the Cherokee Chief, introduced in 1976. This was another Jeep package that combined function and flair. It mounted big tires on wide track axles (65.5-inch track versus 59.2 inches). When equipped with the 401-ci monster V8 and 4.09 gears, this rig could haul the

proverbial tail. Equate it to a powerful, big-engine American station wagon on steroids that grew four-wheel drive.

To meet a public demand, the Cherokee "S" model was expanded in 1977 to include a four-door model. Simple and basic, it had all the convenience of the Wagoneer without the plush trimmings and high cost. The "S" disappeared in 1981, and was replaced by a four-door Cherokee Chief, complete with wide-track axles and stripes. The Cherokee Chief package disappeared after 1982 and was replaced by a similar rig wearing the Cherokee Pioneer name. The big Cherokee line faded out in 1983 to make room for the mid-sized XJ Cherokee.

CHEROKEE XJ: AMC SAVIOR

The midsized Cherokee XJ was a true innovation when it made its debut in 1984. Although it followed a year behind the midsized GM S-10 SUV and made its debut at the same time as the Ford Bronco II, it brought a number of innovations to the market. The first was unibody construction, unique in a nonmilitary 4x4. Many doubted the durability of this construction, but the past 16 years have proven the strength of the design.

Another innovation was the four-link live-axle coil-spring front suspension. It is no exaggeration that this setup, still used in the 2000 TJ Wrangler, XJ Cherokee, and WJ Grand Cherokee, bridged the gap between street manners and trail prowess better than any previous Jeep design and, arguably, better than any other design, period.

The blood transfusion of the XJ line gave AMC the opportunity to put money into developing the Jeep line. One of those developments was the Comanche pickup. The front wrap of the Cherokee was grafted to a rear subframe and a pickup was the result. It was another Jeep move into a growing market, this time the mid-sized pickup. The new truck made its debut in 1986, just in time for the Chrysler purchase. These trucks were later known as the MJ.

Development of the XJ started in the late 1970s when the overwhelming emphasis was on fuel economy. This is why the unibody was developed. The target weight for the project was just under 3,000 pounds and it exceeded this weight only slightly. Power plants were slated to be a new 2.5-liter four and a new 4.0-liter inline six. The four made it to production by 1984, but the six, a complete workover of the old 258-ci AMC six, was delayed. In the interim, AMC Jeep purchased the 2.8-liter V6 from GM, which ironically was the same engine that powered its major competitor in the market, the S-10. This ultimately proved to be a bit of a mistake. The engine was underpowered and not reliable.

The early XJ fielded another engine option, the 1985–1987 Turbo Diesel. This came in response to the many diesel offerings on the market from direct competitors and others. The 126-ci oil burner was made by Renault and offered economy of up to 30 miles per gallon. Like all the other diesel options, the Jeep offering was not overly popular and ended up short-lived. You either love a diesel or you hate it. Evidently most people hated it, because few were sold.

The 4.0-liter six engine put the final brush stroke on the vehicle that could be called a masterpiece. The reliable 258-ci six had been put through a metamorphosis, and the result was a lighter engine with more power and torque. With multiport injection, the first-generation 4.0-liter developed 173 horsepower. Best of all, it could be coupled to a strong but silky smooth four-speed Aisin-Warner automatic.

The Cherokee came in two- and four-door models and featured several variations in trim. The top dollar option was the Wagoneer, which mimicked the old Wagoneer with its plush interior, complete options package, and woodgrain side trim. It was offered as the Wagoneer Brougham, or the ultra-upscale Limited. A pint-size Cherokee Chief was also offered in the two-door line, employing the same trim and graphics of the old big Chief. Cherokee Chief was also offered briefly as a four-door. The Pioneer was the upgrade above the base unit, but below the Wagoneer. In 1985, the Laredo jumped ahead of the Pioneer and continued to be a popular package through the AMC era, and beyond.

At the end of the AMC era, 1986, a new product was brought to the market in the form of the midsized Comanche pickup. Based on the XJ platform, the Comanche made its debut with a 119.6-inch wheelbase and a 7-foot bed. It was later given the code "MJ." With the 2.5-liter, 2.1-liter diesel, or 2.8-liter V6, the Comanche had the same engine choices as the Cherokee. Initially, it was offered in the base Custom trim, the middle road X trim, or the high-scale XLS trim. The Metric Tonne package offered a 2,205-pound capacity. The Fuel Saver package for 4x2 trucks was the ultimate in a baseline model. A sporty 4x2 Eliminator model also rolled out in 1986. The Comanche truck was offered in two- and four-wheel drive and was another Jeep sales tool in the midsized truck wars already raging. Unlike the other Jeep trucks, it survived well into the Chrysler era.

The XJ line brought AMC Jeep back from the brink and provided Chrysler with a springboard to give Jeep a boost after its 1987 purchase.

THE NEW MILLENIUM

CHRYSLER BREATHES NEW LIFE INTO JEEP

Chrysler CEO Lee Iacocca had experience with ailing companies. Having brought Chrysler Corporation back from financial disaster by sheer force of will in the early 1980s, he was confident that the AMC Jeep group could be successfully integrated into the Chrysler organization. AMC was on the rebound at the time of Iacocca's astutely timed purchase, but it was nowhere near healed. Jeep was the healthiest part of the group and what Iacocca had his eyes on. Chrysler needed serious contenders in the developing SUV wars, and Jeep provided a ready and successful source.

The AMC car line was largely scrapped during the takeover, reduced in scope and reorganized into the Eagle line. AMC's manufacturing facilities were utilized to suit the needs of the overall company. Jeep was headlined and Chrysler Corporation began a serious investment in improving quality, adding packages, and optimizing the dealer networks for the Jeep vehicles. As momentum grew, the Jeep line was introduced to Chrysler and Dodge dealers. It proved a good match, since the Chrysler, Dodge, and Jeep lines complemented each other by filling in the gaps. Beyond the hulking Ramcharger, Chrysler was devoid of SUVs. The Jeeps needed to be complemented by a more appealing line of cars.

The Final Edition Grand Wagoneer. The old horse went out in style while still selling well. It died while facing down Corporate Average Fuel Economy Standards (CAFE) and Federal crash standards. The old Grand still has a large following. Only a handful of 1991s were built, making them quite scarce.

s the Jeep operation began hitting on all cylinders, it began to take a larger and larger part of the SUV market, narrowing a 100 percent lead by General Motors to a mere 42 percent in a couple of years. The Jeep line continued its upswing into the early 1990s, when Chrysler delivered Jeep's knockout punch to the SUV world in the form of a new model.

The Ford Explorer had made its debut in 1990 and rocked everyone's SUV sales. Jeep countered in 1993 with the Grand Cherokee. Codenamed the ZJ, this rig combined style with function. It could outperform just about everything in the SUV realm on and off the road. It bridged the gap between street and trail performance just as well or better than anything up to that time. Its only serious contender in that regard was the Range Rover, offered at nearly double the price of the Grand Cherokee.

The early 1990s began with a push by Chrysler to market Jeeps overseas. In England, where the Land Rover had ruled the SUV market for decades with impunity, Jeep quietly took a sales lead. Eventually, a plant was opened in Graz, Austria, to supply Jeeps to Europe and elsewhere. Jeep plant openings followed in Brazil and Argentina, and the company reentered the Japanese, South African, Australian, and Chinese markets in a big way.

The last part of the 1990s brought many refinements, including the coil sprung Wrangler TJ for 1997 and a new Grand Cherokee for 1999. A merger with Daimler of Germany created a new company, Daimler-Chrysler in 1998. That pairing promises to add a completely new dimension to the Jeep world, and time will tell how it will look. A few things are sure: The new millennium promises a new Cherokee and Wrangler. The bottom line is that Jeep is healthier than ever and ready for another 60 years.

WRANGLER YJ: AUTUMN FOR THE LEAF

The YJ, the last fully leaf-spring Jeep, came partly from a need to upgrade the CJ line and partly from political and media pressure. Investigative journalists suddenly realized that a short-wheelbase vehicle with a high center of gravity couldn't be driven like a sports car. This "revelation" brought exposé after exposé and negatively affected Jeep's reputation and sales. To counter, AMC Jeep engineers developed the YJ. If you compare the Wrangler and the old CJ, you will find them close to identical in many ways.

The suspension was modified by adding longer springs, lateral track bars, and anti-roll bars. The axles were widened to increase the track and stability, and the vehicle's ride height was lowered. The final result was a vehicle that was safer and handled better. Some trail prowess was lost, but the loss was easily recoverable with a few easy modifications.

Initially, following the Chrysler takeover, the Wrangler remained much as AMC had left it. The "Wrangler" name on the hood left no doubt that this was *not* a CJ. This 1987 has the Sport Decor group, which included a hood decal, side stripes, and the Convenience Group. The alloy wheels were a separate option.

There were enough cosmetic changes on the Wrangler to make it sorta-kinda look like something new. Creature comforts were improved dramatically with a new interior, and combined with the plush ride, the transition was a good one overall. True Jeep fans fixated on the rectangular headlights and declared them "un-Jeeplike" but Jeepers eventually found the YJ a worthy improvement over the CJ. The press backed off, the corporate image was saved and Jeep life resumed. Thus ensconced, the Wrangler transitioned to Chrysler very soon after its debut.

The Wrangler YJ powertrain changed little over its 1987–1996 run. The venerable 258-ci six stayed on from the CJ and lasted through 1990. For 1991, the 4.0-liter HO engine made its debut. The 2.5-liter four soldiered on

The Renegade made a reappearance in 1991 and was built in limited numbers into 1993. This Renegade had more radical styling than the Renegades of the past, with fender skirts, integrated side steps and bumper skirts, along with 30x9.50 Goodyear Wrangler tires. The 1991 model marked a number of changes, including the addition of the High Output fuel-injected 4.0-liter to the lineup, replacing the old carbureted 258-ci six.

The Wrangler TJ was a technological milestone when it made its debut in 1997. The popular Sahara model made the transition to the coil-sprung TJ as the top of the line unit. A newer shade of the Sage Green color also made the cut. *Jeep*

through the engine era as the base engine, first with a throttle body injection (TBI) system, and then as a silky smooth multi-port with 140 horsepower. From the beginning, the Wrangler had an automatic option: a version of the three-speed Chrysler TorqueFlite. Later units used a lockup torque converter. Manual transmissions were usually five-speeds, but some of the base fours up through 1990 had four-speeds.

One of the bigger mechanical changes from the CJ was the change from a cast-iron gear-drive transfer case from Dana/Spicer to an aluminum chain-

drive unit from New Process (later named New Venture). The front axle was upgraded to a stronger reverse-cut Dana 30 axle and the AMC-20 rear axle was replaced by a Dana 35.

The Wrangler evolved rapidly under Chrysler control by offering more packages. Early in 1987, the line consisted of two packages, the base and the upscale Laredo. Later in the year, the "S" package was introduced, which added a middle-of-the-road level to the Wrangler. The ever-popular Sahara package made its debut in 1987, although it wasn't available until the 1988

The Sport took the middle-of-the-road duties in the TJ line and offered great value. The TJ interior brought great new style and functionality to the Wrangler line. Sales picked up as people discovered how versatile this new rig was in an active, outdoor lifestyle. Even non-four-wheelers valued its sporty, open air fun. The new suspension made it less trucklike and the six gave it plenty of power. *Jeep*

model year. In 1989, the Islander package was added. In 1991, a new version of the Renegade made its debut. With its wide fender flares and integrated bumpers, the Renegade was more street oriented than the Renegades of the past. For 1993, the Islander was replaced by the Sport.

Wrangler YJs were manufactured until 1995. The company produced an extra batch at the end of that year, because when the last one rolled off the Toledo line at the end of the year, the line was converted to producing the new TJ Wrangler. The 1995 YJs filled the gap until the debut of the 1997 TJ in April 1996.

WRANGLER TJ: ALL COILS

Most people would agree the TJ is the best Jeep since Barney Roos built the first one around the Go-Devil engine. With the Quadra-Coil suspension, road and trail performance leaped to new heights. The new coil spring suspension was similar to the type used on the ZJ. It greatly improved both road

The upscale Wagoneer remained in the XJ lineup after the Chrysler takeover. By 1988, it was powered by the 4.0-liter six, a change that gave it best-in-class performance. Chrysler noted decreasing sales of this Jeep variant, while sales of the less opulent XJs were steadily climbing.

Not much had changed cosmetically in the XJ line by 1991, but it still wasn't looking terribly dated. The High Output 4.0-liter made its debut this year and delivered a 13-horsepower increase over the older version.

An XJ version of the Limited made its debut as a mid-year 1987 introduction of the monochromatic styling that Jeep had used since the early 1980s. It has continued, with variations, to this day in the XJ line.

and trail performance. The TJ immediately took the crown as the most capable off-highway vehicle in the United States. It also had round headlights, so it was a true Jeep!

Not only did the TJ receive a new suspension, it also underwent a complete rework of the interior, to include a new dash and Heating Ventilation Air Conditioning (HVAC). In the end, only 23 percent of the YJ's features carried over to the TJ. It may look similar to the YJ, but it's a completely different animal. With the improvement in handling and stability that resulted with the new suspension, plus the airbags, this the safest utility Jeep ever made.

The first TJs were introduced in April 1996 as 1997 models. Until October, only 2.5-liter four-cylinder versions were available. Many people wanted to wait for the 4.0-liter but some couldn't hold out and bought the fours. The

GRAND WAGONEER SJ: LAST OF THE BREED

When Chrysler took over Jeep, the Grand Wagoneer was the oldest unit in the inventory but had one of the staunchest and most loyal customer bases known to man. Similar to AMC, Chrysler scratched its collective head at the continuing popularity of the old workhorse but didn't turn up its nose at the business. Sales remained steady, producing 15,000 units per year until 1990, when the numbers dropped to 10,000. During the last year of Grand Wagoneer production, 1991, only 1,560 units are listed on the production records. These lower numbers are likely from Chrysler cutting back on production rather than a shortage of buyers.

Only a few changes came for the old "Grand" over its last few years. One of the biggest changes was a radical improvement in quality. The last of the Grand Wagoneers are reputed to be the best built of the entire line of Jeeps. People liked the big interior, great visibility and a 5,000-pound tow rating. It reigned as the last of the American big-iron behemoths and for those who missed the good old days, it was a step back in time.

The future is uncertain for the vehicle type that began a half century ago. This 2001 Wrangler TJ is the last link to the crude vehicles of 1940. Will safety mavens and roadless initiative supporters legislate the trail-worthy, short-wheelbase Jeep out of existence? Jeep

trim lineup has remained the base SE, middle Sport, and upper Sahara since the TJ was introduced. Few changes have been made the TJ lineup, and fans of the Jeep would argue that few are needed.

Rumors abound over the ultimate end of the last true Jeep—the only remaining tie to those heady days of 1940. Will the basic short-wheelbase 4x4 fall under the onslaught of the anti-SUV movement? Will the safety mavens kill the concept as "unfit for human consumption"? Will Jeep premiére an emasculated version of the Wrangler? These questions and more all await answers in the new millennium.

The 1994 Country model was the top of the Cherokee line. It had replaced the Wagoneer in that capacity for 1993, when the new Grand Wagoneer made its debut.

A major facelift finally came for the Cherokee in 1997, with the body lines smoothed by integrated bumpers. A new tailgate with hidden hinges and a major interior remake will take the venerable Cherokee to its ultimate end. Hints are that the new generation Cherokees will roll out in 2001. *Jeep*

The success of the Cherokee helped carry the Comanche along. It was a useful and stylish pickup. The old Chief motif reappeared in 1987 and this 1988 Comanche Chief 4x4 has all the goodies, including the sport bar and lights.

The Eliminator package made its debut in 1988 as a sporty 4x2. Four-wheel drive was added to the package in 1990 and the model survived to the end of the line for the Comanche in 1992. Pictured is an 1988 model.

From 1987 on, the only engine available in the Grand Wagoneer was the venerable AMC 360-ci 2-barrel. The manufacture of this engine, virtually a "one-off" for Chrysler, became one of the big nails in the Grand Wagoneer's coffin later in the game. It came down to the fact that this engine was being produced just for the Grand Wagoneer. In fact, many pieces on the vehicle were in that category.

The Corporate Average Fuel Economy (CAFE) was an even bigger consideration. At 11 city and 13 highway EPA rated mileage, the big Jeep was certainly dragging the CAFE average down. While it would have been easy to install a Chrysler engine into the Grand Wagoneer and drag it along for a few more years, it would do nothing for CAFE. If the drag on the CAFE was to be endured, it had best be on one of Chrysler's other, better selling "gas-hogs" like the Ram pickups. The demise of Chrysler's Dodge Ramcharger (EPA 9 city/12 highway miles per gallon) in 1993 came from virtually the same motivations.

The last survivor from the Kaiser era of Jeep rode off into the sunset when the Grand Wagoneer's production ended. Or did it? There is a huge following for the old Grands, especially the well-built Chrysler-era units. A vibrant market exists in the restoration and resale of the remaining models, and they are popular among the rich and famous. The days of American Big Iron lives on!

CHEROKEE XJ: STILL A SAVIOR

The Cherokee XJ was the cornerstone of Jeep sales when Chrysler took over. That year, it had been given its pièce de résistance in the form of the 4.0-liter six and was transformed. With the improvements in build quality that eventually came with the Chrysler takeover, the XJ was perfectly positioned to lead the midsized SUV market. It never quite matched the General Motors midsized SUVs in that regard, but it maintained a healthy segment of the market share and kept GM executives on their toes.

The new management shook up the model line immediately. The Cherokee Limited made its debut in mid-1987 as a four-door with an options package similar to the Wagoneer XJ but with a monochromatic paint scheme available in three colors. In 1988, the two-door Sport package made its debut with an attractive entry level set of options and a sporty look. A two-door version of the Limited also came on the scene that year as the standard Wagoneer departed.

A major innovation from Dana Spicer allows the WJ to attain trail performance far beyond previous limits. The Gerotor system is a trio of special differentials, one in the transfer case and one each in the differentials. They are capable of almost instantly sensing loss of traction and applying torque where needed. The best part is that the system is almost completely transparent. *Jeep*

The 1990 Grand Wagoneer was at the height of opulence in "Grand" and classic style. It was also the most expensive Jeep in the lineup.

The WJ Grand Cherokee carries the Jeep SUV torch into the new millennium. The Laredo name carries on with it. *Jeep*

Laredo was one of the best known of the Jeep designations and a Laredo version of the Grand Cherokee made its debut along with the base model and the top level Limited. The Grand Wagoneer, a wood-sided replacement for both the SJ and XJ variants, was based on the same chassis and was regarded as a separate model. It died after one year.

The fastest ZJ Grand Cherokee ever built was the 1998 5.9-liter Limited. Powered by a 245-horsepower, 360-ci (5.9-liter) V8, it offered truly awesome performance. It was probably the fastest factory SUV ever built. Unfortunately, it was built in limited (pun intended) numbers. *Jeep*

Nothing major changed in the Cherokee lineup until 1993 except for the introduction of the High Output 4.0-liter. With a new "High Port" cylinder head and sequential fuel injection, it pumped out 16 more horsepower than the original "Four-Oh." By 1993, the Cherokee Chief and Pioneer models had departed, but the Cherokee lineup was downsized to make room for the new Grand Cherokee ZJ. With the base two- and four-door units, only the two- and four-door Sport models were available alongside the upscale Country model.

In 1997, the Cherokee received a facelift, and its angular lines were smoothed and softened. In 1998, the "Classic" model was added to the lineup as an upper-middle entry between the base SE, the lower-middle Sport, and the upper scale Limited that had replaced the Country. I guess even a 4x4 knows it's getting long in the tooth when they start calling it a Classic. An updated Cherokee is on the horizon, perhaps by the time you read this book.

Chrysler kept the midsized Comanche MJ pickup around longer than most people would have predicted. It soldiered on until 1992, having gone through a few improvements. Like the XJ, it received the 4.0-liter engine but gained and lost a few trim packages. The Laredo and Chief styles were eliminated in 1989 and replaced with the SporTruck. The Eliminator, formerly available only as a 4x2, was added to the 4x4 line in 1990. The Comanche's production ended after the 1992 model year as the apparent victim of consolidation efforts. It's often said that the Comanche died because it was too much competition for the Dodge Dakota. The Comanche was a good truck, but at its peak it sold only a third of the worst Dakota sales year of the same era.

GRAND CHEROKEE ZJ, WJ

AMC receives credit for beginning the Grand Cherokee project. Code-named the ZJ, it began as a planned replacement for the Cherokee. AMC's

The ZJ handed off to the WJ Grand Cherokee in 1999. They may look like clone brothers, but in fact there are only 127 carryover parts. The WJ uses a smaller, more efficient 4.7-liter V8 that has slightly more power and slightly less torque than the venerable 5.2-liter A-block. The WJ is a bigger machine, though it really doesn't look larger. *Jeep*

financial problems kept development on the slow track until Chrysler came along. When the project was dusted off, Chrysler found a true gem in the making and the ZJ project was soon hitched to a faster locomotive.

Similar to the XJ, the Grand Cherokee was built on a unitized body. It used the Quadra-Coil system that mounted coil springs at all four corners. The base engine was the High Output 4.0-liter six, and the 5.2-liter was available after mid-1993. The ZJ initially had three four-wheel-drive systems available, a part-time system called Command-Trac and two full-time systems: Selec-Trac and Quadra-Trac. The Command-Trac was available only with a five-speed and behind the 4.0-liter six. This combination was discontinued in 1996, and automatic was the only transmission available.

The projected date for the debut of the ZJ was for 1990 or 1991, but the addition of a Chrysler 5.2-liter V8 held off that date. It was determined that there was enough room for a V8, and marketing strategists thought this addition would put the ZJ to the front of the pack. It did go to the front of the pack, and gave the relatively light Grand Cherokee some serious muscles to stretch. The first-generation V8s were capable of going 0 to 60 in under 9 seconds and had a towing capacity of 6,500 pounds. Later versions with the 3.73 rear axle ratio can tow 6,700 pounds and pump out an honest 8.1 second 0 to 60 time. Although the V8 was not available until mid-1993, the prospect of its impending launch enticed many buyers into Jeep dealerships.

The ZJ Grand Cherokee was larger than the XJ but smaller than the old Grand Wagoneer. Initially the Grand Cherokee was offered in three levels, a base model, the Laredo, and the Wagoneer. The Wagoneer was designed to replace both the older SJ-based machine of the same name and the XJ-based unit. It was complete with all the goodies, plus the woodgrain side panels, but it only lasted until 1994.

The Grand Cherokee base model received the "SE" designation in 1994, and the model disappeared in 1996. The Orvis special appeared in 1995 with a rather gaudy two-tone interior and was discontinued in 1996. In 1997, the Tsi, a limited-edition street-oriented model, appeared.

The last year of the ZJ went out with a bang. In 1998, the 5.9-liter Limited appeared and the potent Chrysler 5.9L, 245-horsepower V8 was added to a street-oriented SUV package. The car magazines were dancing in the aisles at the near 7-second 0-to-60 times and the improved handling from the retuned suspension and sticky Goodyear tires. The 5.9-liter overshadowed the other 1998 ZJs that came in the Laredo, Tsi, and Limited trim.

In 1999, the improved Grand Cherokee made its debut and was dubbed the WJ. Jeep said there were only 127 carryover parts from the ZJ. While the WJ carries similar lines to the ZJ, the WJ is wider and longer. Most of the extra space is used to improve the cargo area, formerly filled by the spare tire.

Mechanically, the WJ embodies a great number of improvements. While the 4.0-liter has been retained, it has been tweaked to 195 horsepower. The big news in the engine compartment is the 4.7-liter V8. It produces more power than the 5.2-liter but has a little less torque. It still has enough suds to make the WJ V8 move faster than the V8 ZJ.

Some of the greatest technology improvements are found in the drive-train, where the Dana-Spicer Gerotor pumps replace the center and axle differentials. This system provides a nearly seamless true four-wheel-drive system that can quickly adjust to a variety of traction situations on and off the highway. It isn't foolproof but can easily take the WJ to the practical limits of an SUV-type vehicle on the trail. The WJ puts Jeep on the cutting edge of four-wheel-drive technology and positions Jeep to maintain the lead in the SUV market, perhaps not always in sales but certainly in performance.

CHAPTER 9

WILL THE REAL JEEP PLEASE STAND UP?

JEEP ETYMOLOGY

Jeep® is a famous word, name brand, and trademark. It became an exclusive trademark for Willys-produced vehicles on June 13, 1950, having been filed on February 13, 1943. Willys cited the name as being first used on November 20, 1940. Jeep has been owned and guarded by the succession of corporations that have produced the vehicle ever since, but use of name was not always exclusive to Willys vehicles. In times since the trademark date, use of the name has been strictly monitored, and woe to anyone using the name in vain.

Jeep has entered the general vocabulary, and while it is best known as a brandname, you will find it in most dictionaries in lower case as a noun for a small, sturdy military vehicle. Before we go farther, let's set the ground rules for the use of "Jeep" versus "jeep." In the Jeep world these days, the upper case is used to describe a trademarked vehicle. Technically, that would be one built after the 1950 trademark date, but in common practice, it's used retroactively to describe a post-World War II rig built by Willys. The lower-case word is used to describe the nontrademarked quarter-ton vehicles built by Willys, as well as those built by Ford and Bantam, plus the other non-Jeep jeeps that came before them all.

1947: The Empire "Jeep" Tractor

The Empire tractor was built in small numbers from 1946 to 1948, by the Empire Tractor Company of Philadelphia, Pennsylvania. It utilized a Jeep engine, transmission, transfer case (less the front output), and differential. It was marketed as a low-cost tractor to help set the world back on its agricultural feet after the recent devastating war. Many were sold overseas, but the 4,000 plus units built did not sell as well as hoped and the company faded by the late 1940s. Leftover "New" Empires were sold into the early 1950s at bargain basement prices.

JEEP: THE WORD

Before 1940 and the invention of the vehicle we now know as the Jeep, there were a large number of other definitions of the word jeep. The word was used as a mild 19th century slur (akin to "jerk") among people of German ancestry in the Midwestern United States. There were at least two fairly famous men named Jeep, composer Johann M. Jeep (1582–1650) and author Ludwig Jeep (1846–1911), but there appears to be no connection with either to the quarter-ton vehicle.

The American military connection to the word was formed during World War I, when a "jeep" was either a new, unproven human recruit, or a new, unproven vehicle. This is according to Maj. E. P. Hogan, who wrote a history of the development of the jeep in 1941 for the Army's *Quartermaster Review* magazine. According to Hogan, this term was used in the same context by GIs at the beginning of World War II.

Beyond anecdotes from people alive around the time of World War II, further evidence lies in period publications, such as the December 13, 1941, issue of *Railway Express* magazine. The following caption appears with a photo of a young GI just entering service:

> Private James Smith, like thousands of his fellow recruits, has more than one name these days. He's called "jeep" around camp, "Yard-bird" by the tough Top Sergeant, just "Jimmy" by his sweetheart, and on the payroll he is listed as Private James Smith, U.S. Army. Whatever you call him, he is one of the world's finest fighting men—the kind of soldier the nation proudly depends on in any emergency.

1937: The Boeing B-17 Jeep
One of the most famous aircraft ever built was reportedly known as "Jeep," at least for a time. According to one of the test pilots involved, Col. G. F. Johnson, the prototype YB-17 was called "Jeep" before a newspaper reporter dubbed it the "Flying Fortress." He didn't clarify the reference. *U.S. Air Force Museum*

1938: The Halliburton "Jeep"
In 1936, the Halliburton Oil Well Cementing Company of Duncan, Oklahoma, had been in operation for 17 years. It was a company that made great use of four-wheel-drive trucks, FWDs in particular. That year, FWD built van-bodied 4x4 trucks for exploration. These trucks had the name "Jeep" painted on the sides for reasons that are not immediately clear. This practice continued for several years, even after King Features sent the company a threatening letter. The truck shown is a 1938 four-wheel drive Model HS. A 1941 Model HS truck was photographed with a "Jeep" prominently displayed. *Halliburton*

1940: The Dodge VC "Jeep"

In late 1939, Dodge began building a series of half-ton 4x4 vehicles that earned Dodge a big Army contract and an almost unbroken series of contracts for light-duty 4x4s that lasted into the late 1960s. The VC Series Dodges, especially the Command Car versions, were routinely called "Jeeps" by GIs and period media. The Command Car was the "Jeep" and the quarter-ton was the "Peep." This remained the case into 1942, when the services were inundated by new recruits who had read about quarter-ton jeeps in the papers. The later three-quarter ton Command Cars were unofficially known as "Beeps," for big-Jeeps.

1941: The Curtiss AT-9 Jeep

The AT-9 trainer, also known as the Fledgling, was unofficially called the Curtiss "Jeep," probably for its compact dimensions. Almost 800 were built as a training aircraft for pilots going into multi-engine aircraft. The prototype flew in 1940 and production began in 1941. It had a top speed of 200 miles per hour. Unlike the forgiving quarter-ton jeep, this one had some nasty tricks. It was regarded as a real handful for pilots. Some instructor pilots regarded this as good, because many of the combat aircraft had equally nasty tricks. *U.S. Air Force Museum*

1942: The Minneapolis Moline NTX "Jeep"

While the Army didn't bite on the UTX, the Navy and Marines went for another Minneapolis-Moline product. The NTX was a low-slung 4x4 with a 101-inch wheelbase that was designed for use as an aircraft tug or bomb tractor on rough airfields. Around 1,000 units were built and they saw service mostly in the Pacific Theater. The NTX was called "Jeep" by many. The evidence lies in newspaper clippings, including one from 1943 entitled, "Jeep Helps Save Lives of War Heroes." The story ran a photo of a battered NTX and an account of the Moline tractor dragging a burning aircraft off the runway at Guadalcanal so that out-of-fuel fighters could land. This unit is owned by the Swartzrock Implement Company in Charles City, Iowa.

1942: Aircraft Carrier "Jeeps"
With German U-boats sinking many ships on the Atlantic convoys early in the war, the Navy came up with the Escort Carrier concept. These pint-sized carriers were built on merchant hulls and were about half the size of a regular carrier. They served well in both oceans and were commonly known as "Jeep" carriers. The reference is obviously to the quarter-ton.

1945: The First TJ, Tracked "Jeeps"
While there was an official half-tracked conversion of the MB jeep for use as a snow tractor, this full-tracked and armored prototype was built for the Canadian army. Co-produced by Marmon-Herrington and Willys using many Willys parts, it was dubbed the TJ-1. Five or six prototypes were built that utilized a transverse-mounted Willys engine, transmission, transfer case, and other parts. The unit floated and passed its tests with flying colors. The war ended before it could go into production.

1951: The Toyota "Jeep"

Toyota has grown to rival Jeep in the 4x4 market, but in 1951, it was a fledgling four-wheel drive builder struggling against a war-torn economy and great deal of anger directed its way. Their first commercial model, the BJ, was a small, well-built quarter-ton unit similar in size to the wartime jeep. Like the rest of the world, former enemies or not, the Japanese loved the American jeep. When they named their BJ the Toyota "Jeep," it was with the greatest honorable intent. Their term reflected the type of vehicle rather than a name, but Willys naturally took offense. Thoroughly embarrassed, Toyota renamed the unit "Land Cruiser" and the rest is history.

JEEP: THE CHARACTER

Another appearance of the word *jeep* came in 1936, when a new cartoon character made its debut. On March 16 of that year, Eugene the Jeep made his first appearance in E. C. Segar's "Popeye the Sailor" comic strip. This magical creature who looked like a dog, but walked on his hind legs, was known for saying "Jeep, Jeep!"and became an instant sensation. Eugene could do just about anything and always told the truth. From that point, common slang for something extraordinary was "Jeep." King Features Syndicate filed to make "Jeep" a class 38 cartoon trademark in April 1936. First use was cited as March 26, 1936, and the trademark was granted on August 25, 1936.

JEEP: CONNECT THE DOTS

Go back to 1940. You're a grizzled motor sergeant at Camp Holabird and an extraordinary, but new and unproven vehicle arrives for tests What are you going to call it? Jeep, of course, among other nicknames, including some that are unprintable. Civilian engineers and test drivers hanging around are going to hear it and not understand the military slang. They probably connect to the Eugene the Jeep part, and it fits. History has shown that the quarter-tons had a number of other nicknames, including Peep, Pygmy, Blitz-Buggy, Leapin'

1949: The Davis "Jeep"
This and another 3x2 prototype were delivered for Army tests at the Aberdeen proving ground in April 1949. Built by the Davis Motorcar Company, of Van Nuys, California, they were a spin-off of owner Gary Davis' dream of filling the world with three-wheelers. His ideas died in a storm of controversy and lawsuits. Davis' vehicles were better than his business practices, and the Davis 494X models were tested by the Army with some success. While they did poorly in severe cross-country tests, they did well on the highway and had a particularly supple suspension. They were commonly known as the Davis "Jeeps." Davis was essentially out of business by the time testing was completed in July 1949. This example is owned and was restored by noted military vehicle collector Fred LaPerriere. The second prototype is reported still in existence as well.

OTHER VEHICLES CALLED "JEEP"

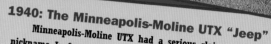

A number of vehicles have been known unofficially or semi-officially as "Jeeps." That doesn't include the still-common usage of the lower case jeep to describe a small, four-wheel-drive vehicle. Most of the vehicles shown here came before the real Jeep took over and in many cases, the term was used as an affectionate nickname. As the Jeep name was trademarked and the vehicles so marked became identified as a product of Willys et al., the practice stopped. After all, by now most of us know what a real Jeep looks like.

1937: The Kellett YG-1 "Jeep"

This rig nearly wore the "Jeep" name officially with the permission of King Features Syndicate, owner of the Popeye copyright. Kellett built autogyros, the 1930s version of the helicopter. By the standards of the day, autogyros were amazing aircraft; able to leap into the air with only a few dozen yards rollout.

The Army was interested in the Kelletts as reconnaissance and artillery spotting aircraft. Test pilot Captain H. F. Gregory was put in charge of the test process. He later became the Army's first helicopter pilot and father of the Army's helicopter service. According to Gregory, who wrote *The Helicopter*, a history of the helicopter, the "Jeep" nickname began around 1937, more than a year into testing.

"You weren't flying an airplane," Gregory wrote. "You weren't flying a helicopter. This craft was in a category of its own. That's why we later nicknamed it 'The Jeep,' and with all due respect to the Ground Forces, the Air Forces has the first Jeep in the Autogyro."

The project went far enough for the Army to buy a squadron and test them in some of the earliest close air support operations; first at Wright Patterson and later elsewhere. Gregory's enthusiastic pilots soon became known as "The Jeep Salesmen."

By 1939, the concept had progressed far enough that the Army was just about ready to buy some autogyros for military use. Kellett had been given official permission to call the YG-1A model the Kellett "Jeep" and to use a caricature of Eugene. Alas, the Army's autogyro project essentially died when Gregory test flew Igor Sikorsky's first helicopter, and so died the Kellett Jeep. Gregory never clarified the exact source for the jeep nickname. Given King Features' involvement, the Eugene influence seems the probable inspiration. *National Archives*

1940: The Minneapolis-Moline UTX "Jeep"

Minneapolis-Moline UTX had a serious claim to the "Jeep" nickname. In fact, during the "Whose Jeep Is It" wars of 1943 and 1948, the Federal Trade Commission officially noted the use of the name in connection to Moline tractors before any of the quarter-ton manufacturers. Had Moline jumped on the same trademark bandwagon that Willys used later, we might know the "Jeep" as a different machine.

The UTX was a variation of one of M-M's big tractors that started development in 1938 as a high-speed artillery tractor. Based on the UDLX Comfortractor, most versions were powered by a 425ci six. It had four-wheel drive, a complete compressed air system, and dual rear tractor tires. A total of six prototypes were built; five with six-cylinder engines and the earliest with a 283ci four. They were a mix of open and closed cabs, and one mounted a .30 caliber machine gun.

According to some sources, the UTX prototypes were tested at the Aberdeen Proving Grounds as early as 1938. Two were lightly tested in July 1939 by the 109th Ordnance Company at Camp Riley, Minnesota. In August 1940, several were put through rigorous tests at Camp Riley during Fourth Army maneuvers and the vehicles earned a great deal of press. Sgt. James T. O'Brien is credited with applying the "Jeep" nickname and as late as 1985, he still cited Eugene as the inspiration for the nickname.

The first article mentioning the new "Jeep" tractor appeared in the August 22, 1940, edition of the *Minneapolis Tribune*, and it received more coverage in the following months that the tractor was called a "Jeep." Army tests went on into 1941 at Aberdeen. After the tests were completed, the Army did not buy into the UTX concept, citing a relatively slow road speed.

The tractor shown is the last UTX survivor and is owned by George Yokiel. The exact history is unclear, but the machine was used in military service. One report says that it was used in Europe, but regardless of the truth, it ended up at Smoky Hill AFB, Kansas, and was "mustered out" right after the war. Wendel Fertig, a Kansas farmer, tried to use it as a tractor, but found it ungainly and parked it. Yokiel purchased it in 1985 and has been slowly rebuilding it, having to reproduce virtually irreplaceable parts.

Lena, Bub, Gnat, Doodle-Bug, Jitterbug, Roller Skate, Struggle-Buggy, and no doubt many others. Peep appears to be the most common, as it appears most often in print during the early part of the 1940s. Some World War II vets, including my father, are still known for using Peep in reference to the World War II quarter-tons. Ample evidence exists that the half-ton Dodge Command Cars were commonly known as jeeps well into 1942.

Writer Fred Lester recently found a dictionary of military slang in the Pentagon Library, *Words of the Fighting Forces* by Clinton A. Sanders, which is dated September 1942. Under "Jeep" the following definition is given:

> Jeep: A four-wheel drive car of one-half to one-and-one-half ton capacity for reconnaissance or other army duty. A term applied the bantam-cars, and occasionally to other motor vehicles (U.S.A.) in the Air Corps, the Link Trainer; in the armored forces, the 1/2 ton command car. Also referred to as 'any small plane, helicopter or gadget!' (U.S.A.A.C.)

JEEP: THE WILLYS INVENTION

One of the biggest initial influences on the Jeep name getting assigned to the Willys quarter-ton was via a newspaper columnist name Kathryn Hillyer. On February 15, 1941, the Quad was driven up the Capitol steps as a publicity stunt and Senate photo op, and was photographed by Sen. James Mead. Hillyer was at the capitol as a reporter for the *Washington Daily News*. Willys test driver Irving "Red" Housman was in the passenger seat and when a bystander asked, "What is this thing?" he replied, "It's a jeep." Hillyer reported this in her syndicated column that appeared around the country.

Willys did a great deal of promotion through its ad agency. Their first Jeep advertisement was shown on December 14, 1941, and appeared in the *Saturday Evening Post*. In successive ads, Willys crowed even more about the jeep. When the company began to take credit for "inventing" the jeep, American Bantam and Minneapolis Moline balked. In 1943, a complaint was filed by the Federal Trade Commission (FTC) against Willys-Overland Motors for unfair trade practices and unfair and deceptive advertising by claiming to be the "inventor" of the jeep. This was only a short time after W-O originally filed papers to trademark the name.

It took the FTC over four years to make a decision that Willys-Overland was to cease and desist in the claims that it originated the jeep concept. The findings acknowledge Willys' contribution toward the perfection of the quarter-ton and allowed it to properly acknowledge those facts in subsequent advertising. This ruling didn't really help Moline or Bantam. They appear to have had no interest in filing for trademark rights to "Jeep," they merely wanted to clarify the facts. By the time the FTC made its ruling, however, the terms Willys and Jeep were so intertwined that it was a moot point. The general public doesn't usually read FTC legal findings, so many people went on believing Willys had invented the jeep, and in many ways, it did. Willys may not have originated the concept, but over many years it, and its progeny, have perfected and redefined the vehicle to the point where you could easily grant that it invented the *civilian* Jeep.

An orphan when it was manufactured, the 1981–1985 Jeep Scrambler CJ is now one of the most popular late model CJs. The longer wheelbase makes it a more stable platform, and its extra room makes it more practical.

THE JEEP LIFESTYLE

PRACTICALLY A RELIGION!

If you want to meet some of the most fanatical vehicle enthusiasts on the globe, attend a Jeep event. If you attend an event and are smart, you won't wear apparel with another 4x4 brand name on it.

Jeep people can be classified into two groups, owners and fanatics. In the case of the former, they appreciate how the vehicle performs. In the latter case they also appreciate the vehicles for what they are. You won't find an owner showing off his Jeep underwear, but in the case of a fanatic, just about anything goes.

The ever-practical Jeep has always been appreciated for what it does, but as time went on, Jeeps acquired an aura, a mystique. World War II was the beginning of that mystique. Millions of GIs and civilians around the world had the chance to see this remarkable machine in action. These witnesses formed the core of the recreational four-wheeling movement that began in the late 1940s and added words such as "Jeepers" and "Jeep-ing" to our vocabulary. Tired war-surplus jeeps were taken over terrain that would have made the sadistic Army test drivers, who tortured the first prototype jeeps at Camp Holabird in 1940, cringe in terror.

Jeep has been very good at combining day to day comfort and convenience with off-highway performance. An ordinary Grand Cherokee can take you to the heights of outdoor pleasure when properly and carefully driven, and do it in comfort.

The Jeep hobby is as broad as the backgrounds of Jeep owners themselves and has tendrils through all walks of life. A Jeep hobbyist can be a person with barely enough income to support his hobby, or he can be a multimillionaire. Execution of the Jeep hobby comes in many forms, from simple use of the vehicle, pristine restorations and collecting, and building up the vehicle to conquer terrifying terrain. The best part is that all the Jeepers get along; each can appreciate the other's form of enjoyment.

RESTORATION

One of the newest Jeep-related hobbies is the restoration of older models. Military jeeps have long been popular in this regard, but in the last 10 years, a growing movement has surfaced and now many older "classic" civilian Jeeps are highly sought-after collectibles. Restored models are entering the collector and classic car show circuits. A restored Jeep now has a chance to compete beside vehicles such as Model J Duesenbergs and Bugattis. Some Jeeps have placed high in the overall competition at the car shows. Some of the classic car enthusiasts have kicked and screamed against it, but when was the last time you saw a Duesenberg fighting on the battlefield to win a world war? That alone should keep the door open for Jeeps at shows.

A Jeep at a car show often draws a great deal of attention. At the recent Circle of the Century car show at Cañon City, Colorado, a car was displayed from each year from 1900 to 2000. Jeeps represented 1942, 1943, and 1944. Guess which rigs were among the most popular at the show? A pair of restored GPWs. Few vehicles have the nostalgia factor that exudes from a World War II jeep. Since these old rigs were used daily, the owner encouraged people to climb on in. To see a piece of history is one thing, but to feel it and smell it is another. The reactions ranged from youthful excitement, to fond remembrance and even a few tears from one veteran.

Besides the military jeeps mentioned above, early CJs built from 1945–1953 are the most popular Jeeps for restoration. The Forward Control models are gaining momentum rapidly for their unusual features. The Jeep Station Wagons and Utility pickups are also very popular because they are more practical than a CJ. Jeepsters were one of the earliest civilian Jeep collectibles, and that market has yet to see a peak. In the modern realm, the 1976–1986 CJ-7 and 1981–1985 CJ-8 are extremely popular because they combine a daily driver with a collector rig. Virtually any older Jeep is a potential collectible.

I would be remiss at this point if I didn't explain the term "restoration." This word has been tossed around and improperly used for decades. A restored vehicle is one that has been brought back to 100 percent original condition, right down to the last nut, bolt, and washer. The quality of the paint and assembly should be no better or worse than what the factory did. In fact,

getting a paint job to match the original on an old jeep can be difficult. Frankly, it's hard to find a painter that will do that poor a job, or an owner that will accept it. Some Jeeps are overrestored and brought up to a standard that the best coachbuilder of the early days would have trouble matching. Overrestoration is a cause for points deducted in judging at shows.

A second level of restoration exists, and that is called "restification." This is a perfect word to describe a lightly modified Jeep that has been essentially restored, but has been slightly modified in some way. It could be a change of tires, a color that wasn't in the original lineup, a few performance mods to the engine, or an extra comfort feature or two. The goal is to make the vehicle more comfortable or usable.

Old Jeeps were simple machines, and one was much like another. For many Jeep restorers, the need to have a unique old Jeep prompts the owner to install period accessories. This is rapidly becoming an obsession with some Jeepers. A rear PTO, Newgren Lift, a set of early Warn hubs, Koenig All-Steel Cab, or even bigger attachments like a Jeep-a-Trench offers a unique appeal. These old accessories are even becoming collectors items themselves.

JEEP EVENTS

The Granddad of the Jeep events is the Jeepers Jamboree. The original event occurred on the notorious Rubicon Trail, high in the Sierra Nevada

One Jeep is not enough for some. Part of Herb Huddle's collection is lined up in front of his barn museum.

Jeeping starts earlier than you think!

Mountains, and it's still an annual event. Mark Smith, a.k.a. "Mr. Jeep," and other members of the Georgetown Rotary Club, held the first Jamboree in 1952 as a means to bring people to the area. In August 1953, the "official" event drew in 55 Jeeps and 150 people. By the 1970s, the number of vehicles had to be limited because of the huge turnout. In just a few years, the Jeepers Jamboree became a big business, and today it is run by a corporation that performs 25 or more events a year around the country and has become home to Jeep's official off-highway driving instructors. Around Jamboree time in Georgetown, California, if you get run over in the street, the odds are almost perfect that the vehicle doing it will be a Jeep!

For many years, Jeeps were the overwhelming favorite among the hard core four-wheeling crowd. Hence the name of certain long-running four-wheeling events, such as the 34-year-old Easter Jeep Safari held by the Red Rock Four Wheelers of Moab, Utah. Other than those organized by Jeep-only clubs, there aren't many Jeep-only events, but Jeep is still the dominant species in nearly any open 4x4 event.

Sometimes jeeps dovetail with another hobby. World War II reenactors and jeeps are a natural combination. These gents are part of the 10th Mountain Division living history show.

PLAYING HARD

Once smitten with the Jeep bug, many owners find they are also infected with a virus we'll call "tinkeritis." In the quest to conquer ever more difficult terrain, modifications are needed. These modifications can range from a few well-chosen additions to major reengineering that produces a vehicle that bears only a faint resemblance to its former self. The farther the Jeep goes up the trail performance food chain, the more modifications are required. At the extreme end, the vehicles become suitable only for the trail environment, and daily beatings are preferable to daily driving. In these cases, the Jeeps are trailered to and from the trail.

Certain Jeep vehicles have proved to be nearly perfect platforms for buildups to transit hard-core terrain. The Jeep CJ, Wrangler YJ, and TJ have the ideal dimensions to squeeze through and drive over anything in their path, but that's not to say that other Jeeps won't work. The Cherokee XJ is another popular builder. It's light, compact, and has a flexible suspension and good drivetrain. However, it's more vulnerable to damage and difficult to repair. Even the luxury Grand Cherokee is modified for trail use by owners who want to have their cake and eat it too.

A military jeep may provide a link with someone who paid the ultimate sacrifice.

One of the perennial favorites of the four-wheeling crowd is the flatfender Jeep. Over the past 50 years, a great database has been compiled on building these compact Jeeps. For maximum effect, as Tom Telford demonstrates with his highly modified 1959 CJ-3B.

Even the Jeep SUVs are capable of conquering some very serious terrain, as Billy Vickers demonstrates with his 1993 Grand Cherokee.

Mike Palmer's radical 1951 M-38 is one step short of a full-blown, dedicated rock buggy. Very little of the original Jeep remains, but the fact that it still uses the original chassis keeps it out of that category. This vehicle shows the battle scars of years of extreme four-wheeling.

The CJ-7 and Wrangler are generally considered by many to be the perfect combination of wheelbase and compact dimensions for the trail. A very short wheelbase can be tricky. The longer rigs are slightly more stable and have more room for people and gear. Doug Engel's 1983 CJ-7 has had about $30,000 worth of modifications.

AMBASSADOR JEEP

It's interesting to note that during World War II, the Jeep was one of America's best ambassadors. A jeep powered an olive oil plant in starving, war-torn Italy. A jeep carried a pregnant German woman through a soggy winter landscape to an American aid station so she could give birth in a warm, safe, and clean environment. Jeeps helped an English farmer get his fields plowed and planted. All of these incidents, and thousands of others, connected the basic goodwill of the American people to the battered little vehicle they drove.

Today, the ambassadorial work of the Jeep has opened doors on a purely human level. How many times has, "Nice Jeep," opened the door to a conversation among strangers? In any language, the word "Jeep" receives instant understanding. Countries accustomed to heaping abuse on America and Americans love the Jeep. How many times have you seen news footage of enraged inhabitants of some country burning our flag and our current president in effigy while a Jeep is parked in the background. "Yankees go home, but leave your Jeeps!"

The Jeep went from a single slapped-together pilot model built by a company with one foot in the grave to a vast line of sleek, superbly engineered all-wheel-drive vehicles built by a successful, mega-million dollar company in just 60 years. Who would have thought? The times are a-changin', but there always seems to be a spot in this world for America's favorite four-letter four-by. . . . Jeep.

159

GLOSSARY:
THE JEEP ALPHABET

From almost the beginning, Jeep models were given a pair of code letters. They changed a bit over the years and weren't always consistent, but knowing the terms puts you a step higher on the Jeep history food chain. What follows is a listing of most commonly known Jeep models, production or not, from 1941 to the present, and their factory code letters. The military M-series designations for rigs not given a model code are also included.

AJ: A military jeep concept from about 1950. AJ probably stood for "Advanced Jeep." It's not certain that a pilot model was ever built.

BC: A pilot model military lightweight Jeep built in 1953 and nicknamed the "Bobcat."

BRC-40: The Bantam pre-standardized jeeps. Built in 1941.

BRC-60: The Bantam quarter-ton prototypes. Built 1940–1941.

C-101: The Jeepster Commando. Built from 1966 to 1971.

C-104: The second incarnation of the Commando, built 1972–1973 after AMC acquired Jeep. Technically, only the 1973 is a C-104.

CJ: For "Civilian Jeep." Built from 1944–1986. A.k.a. the "Junior" line.

CJ-V35/U: A special waterproofed version of the CJ-3A built for the U.S. Navy in 1950.

CJ-1: The first pilot model civilian Jeeps in early 1944 were called CJ-1s. They were modified MB models.

CJ-2: The second batch of CJs were called CJ-2s. They were prototypes built from scratch in 1944 and 1945.

CJ-2A: The first production CJ, built from 1945 and into 1949.

CJ-3A: Built from 1949 through 1953.

CJ-3B: The "high-hood" flatfender. Built from 1953 to 1968 by Willys and currently being produced under license in other countries.

CJ-4: A prototype vehicle that led to the CJ-5. Built 1950 or 1951.

CJ-4A: The original designation for the CJ-3B while it was experimental.

CJ-4M: A pilot model military Jeep from about 1950 that mounted an F-head engine. Led to the model MD.

CJ-4MA: A long-wheelbase pilot model/prototype ambulance from about 1951 that led to the model MDAs.

CJ-5: The "round-fender" Jeep built from 1955 through 1983.

CJ-5A: The 1964–1967 Tuxedo Park Mark IV, based on the CJ-5.

CJ-5.5: The experimental designation for the CJ-7 from around 1972.

CJ-6: A long-wheelbase variant of the CJ-5. Built from 1955 to 1976 for domestic use and to 1981 for export.

CJ-6A: The 1964–1967 Tuxedo Park Mark IV based on the CJ-6.

CJ-7: A longer version of the CJ-5 with hard doors and more comfort. Built in large numbers from 1976–1986.

CJ-8: A.k.a. the Scrambler. A long-wheelbase pickup variant of the CJ-7. Built from 1981 to 1986.

CJ-10: An export truck that resembled a CJ. Built 1982–1984.

CJ-10A: A short, 4x2 version of the CJ-10 built by AM General as a military aircraft tug.

DJ: The 4x2 "Dispatcher." Built in several versions from 1956.

DJ-3A: Built from 1956 through 1964. A 4x2 based on the CJ-3A and built in several variations, including postal versions.

DJ-5: A 4x2 based on the CJ-5 and built 1965–1983 by Jeep and later by AM General. From 1965 to 1972, they were available as both a standard Jeep and as a hard cab postal model, but from there they became commercial only as postal units. Each new postal model got a new designation like DJ-5A, B, C, etc. The DJ-5L was the last produced under AMC control.

FC: For "Forward Control." Cabover trucks. Built 1957–1965 in two wheelbase lengths.

FC-150: The short-wheelbase Forward Control.

FC-170: The long-wheelbase Forward Control.

FJ: The code letters for a series of step vans built on various Jeep chassis and called the Fleetvan.

FJ-3: The postal version of the 4x2 Fleetvan. Based on the DJ-3A chassis.

FJ-3A: The commercial version of the 4x2 Fleetvan.

FJ-6: An updated Fleetvan based on the DJ-6 chassis built from 1965 into the 1970s. Other FJs were built, the FJ-9, for example, came around 1975 and was based on the Jeep truck chassis.

GP: The Ford pre-standardized quarter-tons that followed the "Pygmy"; G = Government Contract, P = 80-inch Reconnaissance car. Built only in 1941.

GPA: The Ford-built amphibious jeep. G = Government Contract, P = 80-inch Reconnaissance car, A=amphibian. Built 1942–1943. A.k.a. the "Seep."

GPW: The Ford-built World War II jeep built to the standardized design. G = Government Contract, P = 80-inch Reconnaissance car, W = Willys engine. Built 1942–1945.

MA: The Willys pre-standardized quarter-ton that followed the "Quad," M = Military contract, A = series. Built only in 1941.

MB: Standardized Willys quarter-ton jeep of World War II. M = Military contract, B = series. Built 1942–1945.

MB-T: The "Super Jeep" 6x6 prototypes. A.k.a. "Tug." Sixteen were built in 1943.

MC: The first post-World War II military variant of the jeep. A.k.a. the M-38. M = Military contract, C = series. Built 1950–1955.

MD: The second major offshoot of the original jeep and the basis for the CJ-5. A.k.a. the M-38A1. M = Military contract, D = series. Built most years 1952–1971, though many of the later production rigs went to foreign markets.

MDA: The long-wheelbase version of the MD, known as the M-170. These rigs were built in small numbers as needed from 1954 to 1967.

MJ: The pickup variant of the XJ Cherokee. Built from 1986–1992.

M-38: See "MC."

M-38A1: See "MD."

M-38A1C AND D: See "MD."

M-38E1: A prototype version of an F-head-engine-powered military Jeep. A.k.a. the CJ-4M.

M-151: The Military Utility Tactical Truck (M.U.T.T.). Designed by Ford under a military contract, but built in large numbers by Willys and AM General. M-151A1 and M-151A2 were upgrades.

M-170: See "MDA."

M-422: The "Mighty-Mite" built by American Motors 1960–1963. The M-422A1 was the longer-wheelbase version. Not a true Jeep, but a cousin.

M-606: A militarized export version of the CJ-3B built from the 1950s into 1968. The M-606A1 was a 24-volt variant.

M-606A2: A militarized export version of the CJ-5 built from 1968 to 1971. The M-606A3 was the 24-volt variant.

M-676: The military Forward Control pickup built 1963–1964. Based on the FC-170.

M-677: The military Forward Control crew-cab pickup built 1963–1964. Based on the FC-170.

M-678: The military Forward Control van/carryall built 1963–1964. Based on the FC-170.

M-679: The military Forward Control ambulance built 1963–1964. Based on the FC-170.

M-715: The military cargo version of the J-Series Gladiator built late 1966–1969. The AM-715 was a later export variant built by AM General.

M-718: An ambulance version of the M-151.

M-725: The military ambulance version of the J-Series Gladiator built 1967–1969.

M-729: The military utility-bodied version of the J-Series Gladiator built 1967–1969.

M-825: An M-151 specially built to carry a TOW missile.

SJ: The Wagoneer SUV or Gladiator (J-Series) pickup. A.k.a. the "Senior" line, or as "Big Jeeps." Big Wagoneers were built from 1963 to 1991 and trucks from 1963 to 1987.

TJ: The latest coil sprung Wrangler variant introduced for 1997 and still in production.

TJ-1: The military tracked jeep prototypes built 1944–1945.

VJ: The first Jeepster, a 4x2. Built 1949–1950.

WJ: The updated Grand Cherokee that appeared in 1999 and is still in production.

XJ: The mid-sized Cherokee line introduced for 1984 and still in production.

YJ: The Wrangler. Built from 1987 to 1997.

ZJ: The Grand Cherokee line, built 1993–1999.

APPENDIX 1: SUGGESTED READING

Ackerson, Robert C. **Standard Catalog of 4x4s, 1945–1993.** Iola, Wisconsin: Krause Publications, Inc., 1993.

Allen, Jim. **Illustrated Classic 4x4 Buyer's Guide.** Osceola, Wisconsin: MBI Publishing Company, 1997.

Allen, Jim. **Illustrated Jeep Buyers Guide**. Osceola, Wisconsin: MBI Publishing Company, 1999.

Berndt, Thomas. **Standard Catalog of U.S. Military Vehicles, 1940–1965.** Iola, Wisconsin: Krause Publications, Inc., 1993.

Clarke, R. M. **Off Road Jeeps Civilian & Military, 1944–1971.** Surrey, England: Booklands Books Ltd.

Clayton, Michael. **Jeep.** North Pomfret, Vermont: David & Charles Inc., 1982.

Cowdery, Ray. **All-American Wonder** Volume One. Lakeville, Minnesota: USM, Inc., 1993.

Cowdery, Ray. **All-American Wonder** Volume Two. Lakeville, Minnesota: USM, Inc., Northstar Books Division; 1990.

Crismon, Fred W. **U.S. Military Wheeled Vehicles.** Osceola, Wisconsin: MBI Publishing Company, 1994.

Foss, Christopher F. **Military Vehicles of The World.** New York: Charles Scribner's Sons, 1976.

Foster, Patrick R. **The Story of Jeep.** Iola, Wisconsin: Krause Publications, Inc., 1998.

Mroz, Albert. **Illustrated Encyclopedia of American Trucks and Commercial Vehicles.** Iola, Wisconsin: Krause Publications, 1996.

Post, Dan R. **American Bantam Maintenance Manual, TM10-1205.** Arcadia, California: Post-Era Motorbooks, 1971.

Rifkind, Herbert R. **Jeep Genesis.** London, England: ISO Publications, 1988.

Sampietro, A. C. and K. G. Matthews. **The New Overhead Camshaft Willys Engine.** New York: Society of Automotive Engineers, Inc., 1962.

Sessler, Peter C. **Jeep, 1941–2000 Photo Archive.** Hudson, Wisconsin: Iconografix, 2000.

Statham, Steve. **Jeep Color History.** Osceola, Wisconsin: MBI Publishing Company, 1999.

— . **Maintenance Manual for Willys Truck, 1/4 Ton 4x4 Model MB.** Toledo, Ohio: Willys-Overland Motors, Inc., 1942.

— . **The Complete WW2 Military Jeep Manual.** Andover, New Jersey: Portrayal Press.

— . **U.S. Army Military Vehicles WW2.** Surrey, England; Portrayal Press, Brooklands Books Ltd., (reprint of 1943 TM 9-2800).

APPENDIX 2: SELECTED SPECIFICATIONS

Bantam BRC-40, 1941

Engine

Type	4-cylinder L-head (Continental Model BY 4112)
Displacement	112 ci
Bore and Stroke	3.20x3.50 in
Power	45 hp @ 3,500 rpm
Torque	86 ft-lbs @ 1,800 rpm
Compression Ratio	6.8:1

Transmission

Type and Model	3-speed, Warner Gear T-84D (ASI-T84-H)

Transfer Case

Type and Model	2-speed, Spicer Model 18 (#001865)

Axles

Front Type and Model	Full-floating, Spicer Model 40 (#2046R)
Rear Type and Model	Full-floating, Spicer Model 40 (#2047R)
Ratios (std/opt)	4.88:1

Dimensions and Capacities

Wheelbase	79 in
Approach Angle	45 deg
Departure Angle	30 deg

Willys Model MA, 1941

Engine

Type	4-cylinder L-head (Willys 441 or 442)
Displacement	134.2 ci
Bore and Stroke	3.12x4.37 in
Power	60 hp @ 4,000 rpm
Torque	105 ft-lbs @ 2,000 rpm
Compression Ratio	6.48:1

Transmission

Type and Model	3-speed, Warner Gear T-84J

Transfer Case

Type and Model	2-speed, Spicer Model 18

Axles

Front Type and Model	Full-floating, Spicer Model 25
Rear Type and Model	Full-floating, Spicer Model 23-2
Ratios (std/opt)	4.88:1

Dimensions and Capacities

Wheelbase	80 in
Curb or Shipping Weight	2,150 lbs
Gross Vehicle Weight	2,800 lbs
Fuel Capacity	10 gal

Ford GP, 1941

Engine

Type	4-cylinder L-head (Ford GP)
Displacement	119 ci
Bore and Stroke	3.185x3.75 in
Power	45 hp @ 3,600 rpm
Torque	84 ft-lbs @ 2,000 rpm
Compression Ratio	6.9:1

Transmission

Type and Model	3-speed, Ford GP-7000

Transfer Case

Type and Model	2-speed, Spicer Model 18

Axles

Front Type and Model	Full-floating, Spicer Model 25
Rear Type and Model	Full-floating, Spicer Model 23-2
Ratios (std/opt)	4.88:1

Dimensions and Capacities

Wheelbase	80 in
Length x Width x Height	127.85 x 60.52 x 40.0 in
Curb Weight	2,150 lbs
Gross Vehicle Weight	2,140 lbs
Fuel Capacity	10 gal

MB GPW, 1941–1945

Engine

Type	4-cylinder L-head
Displacement	134.2 ci
Bore and Stroke	3.13x4.38 in
Power	60 hp @ 4,000 rpm
Torque	105 ft-lbs @ 2,000 rpm

Transmission

Type and Model	3-speed, Warner Gear T-84J

Transfer Case

Type and Model	2-speed, Spicer Model 18

Axles

Front Type and Model	Full-floating, Spicer 25
Rear Type and Model	Full-floating, Spicer 23-2
Ratios (std/opt)	4.88:1

Dimensions and Capacities

Wheelbase	80 in
Length x Width x Height	132.75 x 62 x 69.75
Curb Weight	2,315 lbs
Gross Vehicle Weight	3,125 lbs
Fuel Capacity	15 gal

GPA, 1942–1943

Engine

Type	4-cylinder L-head
Displacement	134.2 ci
Bore and Stroke	3.13x4.38 in
Power	60 hp @ 4,000 rpm
Torque	105 ft-lbs @ 2,000 rpm

Transmission

Type and Model (copy of Warner T-84)	3-speed, Ford Model GPW 7000

Transfer Case

Type and Model (copy of Spicer 18)	2-speed, Ford Model GPW 7700

Axles

Front Type and Model (copy of Spicer 25)	Full-floating, Ford Model GPW 3001
Rear Type and Model (copy of Spicer 23-2)	Full-floating, Ford Model GPW 4001
Ratios (std/opt)	4.88:1

Dimensions and Capacities

Wheelbase	84 in
Length x Width x Height	181.83 x 64 x 69 in
Curb or Shipping Weight	3,400 lbs
Gross Vehicle Weight	4,450 lbs
Fuel Capacity	15 gal

CJ-2A, 1946–1949
CJ-3A, 1949–1953
CJ-3B, 1953–1964

Engine

	CJ-2A/CJ-3A	CJ-3B
Type	4-cylinder L-head	4-cylinder F-head
Displacement	134.2 ci	134.2 ci
Bore and Stroke	3.13x4.38 in	3.13x4.38 in
Compression Ratio	6.48:1	6.9:1 (7.4:1)
Power	63 hp @ 4,000 rpm	75 hp @ 4,000 rpm
Torque	105 ft-lbs @ 2,000 rpm	114 hp @ 2,000 rpm

Transmission

	CJ-2A/CJ-3A	CJ-3B
Type and Model	3-speed Warner T-90	3-speed Warner T-90C

Transfer Case

Type and Model	2-speed, Spicer Model 18R

Axles

Front Type and Model	FF, Spicer Model 25
Rear Type and Model	FF, Spicer Model 23-2 (1945–early 1946 CJ-2A to SN 13453)
	SF, Spicer Model 41-2 (1946–1949 CJ-2A)
	SF, Spicer Model 44-2 (1949-up CJ-3A and CJ-3B)
Ratios (std/opt)	5.38:1

Dimensions and Capacities

	CJ-2A	CJ-3A	CJ-3B
Wheelbase	80 in	80 in	80 in
Length x Width x Height	130.8 x 59 x 69 in	129.75 x 59 x 66.75in	130 x 59 x 66.25in
Curb Weight	2,215 lbs	2,205 lbs	2,243 lbs
Gross Vehicle Weight	3,500 lbs	3,500 lbs	3,500 lbs
Fuel Capacity	10.5 gal	10.5 gal	10.5 gal

M-38, 1950–1952
M-38A1, 1952–1957
M-170, 1953–1957

Engine

	M-38	M-38A1/M-170
Type	4-cylinder L-head	4-cylinder F-head
Displacement	134.2 ci	134.2 ci
Bore and Stroke	3.13x4.38in	3.13x4.38 in
Compression Ratio	6.48:1	6.9:1
Power	60 hp @ 4,000 rpm	72 hp @ 4,000 rpm
Torque	105 ft-lbs @ 2,000 rpm	114 ft-lbs @ 2,000 rpm

Transmission

Type and Model	3-speed, Warner T-90

Transfer Case

Type and Model	2-speed, Spicer Model 18

Axles

Front Type and Model	FF, Spicer Model 25
Rear Type and Model	SF, Spicer Model 44-2 (1949-up CJ-3A and CJ-3B)
Ratios (std/opt)	5.38:1

Dimensions and Capacities	M-38	M-38A1/M-170
Wheelbase	80 in	81 in/101 in
Length x Width x Height	133 x 62 x 74in	139 x 61 x 74in/155 x 60.5 x 80in
Curb Weight	2,750 lbs	2,660 lbs/2,963 lbs
Gross Vehicle Weight	3,950 lbs	3,865 lbs/3,763 lbs
Fuel Capacity	13 gal	17 gal/20 gal

M-715 series, 1967–1969

Engine

Type	6-cylinder OHC
Displacement	230 ci
Bore and Stroke	3.44x4.37 in
Compression Ratio	7.5:1
Power	132.5 hp @ 4,000 rpm
Torque	198 ft-lbs @ 1,700 rpm

Transmission

Type and Model	4-speed, Warner T-98

Transfer Case

Type and Model	2-speed, NP-200

Axles

Front Type and Model	FF, Dana 60
Rear Type and Model	FF, Dana 90
Ratios (std/opt)	5.87:1

Dimensions and Capacities	M-715	M-725/M-729
Wheelbase	126 in	126 in
Length x Width x Height	209 x 85 x 85 in	210 x 85 x 95 in
Curb Weight	5,500 lbs	6,400 lbs
Gross Vehicle Weight	8,900 lbs	8,900 lbs
Fuel Capacity	30 gal	30 gal

CJ-5, CJ-6, 1955–1971

Engine

	Std.	Opt.		Opt.
Type	4-cylinder	F-head	V6 OHV	4-cylinder OHV diesel
Displacement	134.2 ci	225 ci		192.2 ci
Bore and Stroke	3.14 x 4.38 in	3.7 5x 3.40 in		3.5 x 5.0 in in
Compression Ratio	6.7:1 (7.1:1*)	9.0:1		16.5:1
Power	72 (75*) hp @ 4,000 rpm	160 hp @ 4,200 rpm		62 hp @ 3,000 rpm
Torque	114 ft-lbs (117*) @ 2,000 rpm	230 ft-lbs @ 2,400 rpm		143 ft-lbs @ 1,350 rpm
	* High Compression			

Transmission

	3-speed	4-speed
Type and Model	Warner T-90C (F-134)	Warner T-98 (F-134)
Warner T-14A (V6)		

Transfer Case

Type and Model	2-speed, Spicer Model 18

Axles

Front Type and Model	Spicer 25 (1955-1965)
Spicer 27 (1966-1971)	
Rear Type and Model	Spicer 44-2
Ratios (std/opt)	4.27/4.88/5.38 (F-134)
3.73/4.88 (V6)	

Dimensions and Capacities	CJ-5	CJ-6
Wheelbase	81 in	101 in
Length x Width x Height	135.5 x 71.7 x 69.5 in	155.5 x 71.7 x 68.4 in
Curb Weight	2,274 lbs (F-134)	2,336 lbs (F-134)
	2,351 lbs (V6)	2,413 lbs (V6)
Gross Vehicle Weight	3,750 lbs	3,900 lbs
Fuel Capacity	10.5 gal	10.5 gal

CJ-5, CJ-6, CJ-7, CJ-8, 1972–1986

Engine

	4-cylinder	6-cylinder	V8
Type	Inline OHV	Inline OHV	OHV
Displacement	151 ci (GM, 1980-1983)	232 ci (std)	304 ci (opt 1972-1981)
	150 ci (AMC, 1984-up)	258 ci (opt)	
Bore and Stroke	4.00x3.00 in (GM)	3.75x3.50 in	3.75x3.44 in
Compression Ratio	8.2:1 (GM)	8.5:1	8.4:1
	9.2:1	8.4:1	
Power	82 hp @ 4,000 rpm	145 hp@ 4,300 rpm	150 hp @ 4,200 rpm
	105 hp @ 5,000 rpm	115 hp @ 3,200 rpm	
Torque	125 ft-lbs @ 2,600 rpm	215 ft-lbs @1,600 rpm	245 ft-lbs @ 2,500 rpm
	132 ft-lbs @ 2,800 rpm	210 ft-lbs @1,800 rpm	

Transmission

	3-speed	4-speed	Automatic
Type and Model	1 Warner T-14A	Warner T-18	GM TH-400 (CJ-7)
	(std, I-6,1972–1975)	(opt I-6, 1972–1975)	(opt V8, 1976–1979)
	2 Warner T-15	Warner T-18A	Chrysler 904
	(std V8, 1972–1975)	(opt I-6, 1976–1986)	(opt I-4, 1981–1986)
	3 Tremec T-150	Tremec T-176	Chrysler 999
	(std I-6 , 1976–1979)	(std I-6, 1980–1986)	(opt I-6, V8, 1980–1986)
	(Std V8, 1980–81)		
	4	Borg Warner SR-4	
		(std I-4, 1980–1981)	
	5	Borg Warner T-4	
		(std I-4, 1982–1986)	
	6	5-Speed, Borg Warner T-5	
		(opt I-4, I-6, 1982–1986)	

Transfer Case

	1972–1979	1980–1986
Type and Model	2-speed, Dana 20	2-speed, Dana 300
(manual trans)		
2-speed, BW1339 full-time		

Axles

Front Type and Model	FF, Dana 30
Rear Type and Model	SF, Dana 44 (1972–1975 and late 1986)
SF, AMC 20 (1976–1986)	
Ratios (std/opt)	3.73/4.27 (1972–1975)
3.54/4.10 (1976–1979)	
3.07/3.54, 3.73 (1980–1982 I6 and V8)	
3.54/4.09 (1980–1986 I-4)	
2.73/3.54, 3.73 (1980–1986 I-6)	

Dimensions and Capacities	CJ-5	CJ-6	CJ-7
Wheelbase	83.5 in	103.5 in	93.5 in
Length x Width x Height	134.8 x 68.6 x 71.4	158.4 x 59.9 x 67.6	144.3 x 68.6 x 70.5
Curb Weight	2,789 lbs (V8)	2,743lbs	2,952 lbs (V8)
Gross Vehicle Weight	3,755 lbs(4,155)	3,900 lbs	3,755 lbs(4,155)
Fuel Capacity	15.5 gal	15.5 gal	15.5 gal (20.0 gal opt)

	CJ-8
Wheelbase	103.5 in
Length x Width x Height	177.3 x 68.6 x 71.4 in
Curb Weight	2,701 lbs
Gross Vehicle Weight	4,155 lbs
Fuel Capacity	15.5 gal (20.0 gal opt)

Willys 4x4 Station Wagons, 1949–1965
Willys 4x4 Panel Deliverys, 1953–1965
Willys 4x4 Trucks, 1947–1965

Engine	4-63 Models	4-73/75 Models
Type	4-cylinder L-head	4-cylinder F-head
Displacement	134.2 ci	134.2 ci
Bore and Stroke	3.13x4.38 in	3.13x4.38 in
Compression Ratio	6.48:1(7.1:1 opt)	6.9:1 (7.4:1 opt)
Power	63 hp @ 4,000 rpm	75 hp @ 4,000 rpm
Torque	105 ft-lbs @ 2,000 rpm	114 ft-lbs @ 2,000 rpm

	6-226 Models	6-230 Models
Type	6-cylinder L-head	6-cylinder OHC
Displacement	226.2 ci	230 ci
Bore and Stroke	3.31x4.38 in	3.34x4.38 in
Compression Ratio	6.86:1 (7.3:1)	8.5:1 (7.5:1)
Power	115 hp @ 3,850 rpm	140 hp @ 4,000 rpm (133 hp @ 4,000 rpm)
Torque	190 ft-lbs @ 1,800 rpm	210 ft-lbs @ 1,750 rpm
		(199 ft-lbs @ 2,400 rpm)
Torque	190 ft-lbs @ 1,800 rpm	2-bbl Holley

Transmission	Wagons	Truck
Type and Model	3-speed Warner T-90	3-speed Warner T-90E
Ratios	1: 2.80, 2: 1.55, 3: 1.00, R: 3.80	1: 3.34, 2: 1.85, 3: 1.00, R: 4.53

Axles	Wagons	Truck
Front Type and Model	FF, Spicer 25	FF, Spicer 25
Rear Type and Model	SF, Spicer 41-2	SF, Timken 51540
	SF, Spicer 44 (6-226)	
Ratios (std/opt)	5.38:1 (4-cylinder)	5.38:1/6.17:1
4.88:1/5.38 (6-cylinder)		

Dimensions and Capacities	Wagons	Truck
Wheelbase	104 in (104.5 in after 1955)	118 in
Length x Width x Height	176.25 x 68.81 x 72.75 in	182.5 x 73.16 x 74.5 in
Curb Weight	3,278 lbs (SW)	3,331 lbs (4-63 pickup)
3,365 lbs (Panel)		
Gross Vehicle Weight	4,500 lbs	4,700 lbs(4-63 HT)
5,300 lbs (4-63)		
Fuel Capacity	15 gal	15 gal

FC-150, FC-170, 1957–1965

Engine			
Type	4-cylinder F-head	6-cylinder L-head	3-cylinder OHV diesel
Displacement	134.2 ci	226.2 ci	170 ci
Power	72 hp @ 4,000 rpm	105 hp @ 3,600 rpm	85 hp @ 3,000 rpm
Torque	115 lb-ft @ 2,000 rpm	190 lb-ft @ 1,400 rpm	170 lb-ft @ 1,900 rpm
Compression Ratio	6.9:1 (7.4:1 opt)	6.86:1 (7.3:1 opt)	22:1

Transmission	Std (FC-150, 170, M-series)	Opt (FC-170)
Type and Model	3-speed, Warner T-90	4-speed, Warner T-98

Transfer Case	
Type and Model	2-speed, Spicer Model 18

Axles	FC-150	FC-170	FC-170DRW
Front Type and Model	Spicer 25 (to 1958)	Spicer 44F	Spicer 44F
Spicer 44F			
Rear Type and Model	Spicer 44	Spicer 53	Spicer 70
Ratios (std/opt)	5.38:1	4.88:1	4.88:1

Dimensions and Capacities	FC-150	FC-170
Wheelbase	81 in	103.5 in
Length x Width x Height	147.4 x 71.4 x 77.4 in	180.5 x 76.5 x 79.4 in
	184.3 x 78 x 91 in(M-series)	
Curb Weight	3,273 lbs	3,490 lbs
		4,841 lbs (DRW)
Gross Vehicle Weight	5,000 lbs	7,000 lbs
		8,000 lbs (DRW 3-speed)
		9,000 lbs (DRW 4-speed)
Fuel Capacity	16 gal	22 gal

Wagoneer and Gladiator, 1963–1970

Engine	6-Cylinder	6-Cylinder
Type	6-cylinder OHC	6-cylinder OHV
Displacement	230 ci	232 ci
Bore and Stroke	3.44x4.37 in	3.75x3.50 in
Compression Ratio	8.5:1	8.5:1
Power	140 hp @ 4,000 rpm	145 hp @ 4,300 rpm
Torque	210 lb-ft @ 1,700 rpm	215 lb-ft @ 1,600 rpm

	V8	V8
Type	V8 OHV	V8 OHV
Displacement	327 ci	350 ci
Bore and Stroke	4.00x3.25 in	3.80x3.85 in
Compression Ratio	8.7:1/9.7:1	9.0:1
Power	250 hp @ 4,700 rpm	230 hp @ 4,400 rpm
	270 hp @ 4,700 rpm	
Torque	340 lb-ft @ 2,600	350 lb-ft @ 2,400 rpm
	360 lb-ft @ 2,600 rpm	

Transmission	3-speed	4-speed	Automatic
Type and Model	1 Warner Gear T-90A	Warner Gear T-98	Borg Warner AS-8W
	(std OHC-6, 1963–1965)	(opt trk, 1964–1967)	(opt, 1963–1965)
	2 Warner Gear T-85	Warner GearT-18	GM TH-400
	(std V8, 1963–67)	(opt, 1968–1970)	(opt V8, 1965–1970)
	3 Warner Gear T-14A		
	(std I-6, 1965–1970)		
	4 Warner Gear T-15A		
	(std V8, 1968–1970)		

Transfer Case	Manual	Automatic
Type and Model	2-speed Spicer 20	1-speed Spicer 21 (into 1965)

Axles	Wagoneer	Truck
Front Type and Model	FF, Spicer 27AF	FF, Spicer 44F
IFS, Spicer 27IFS (opt)	IFS, Spicer 44	IFS (opt)
Rear Type and Model	SF, Spicer 44	SF, Spicer 44 (4,000–5,500 GVW)
		SF, Spicer 53 (5,600–7,000 GVW)
		FF, Spicer 60 (6,000–7,000 GVW)
		FF, Spicer 70 DRW (7,600–9,000 GVW)
Ratios (std/opt)	3.73 (4.09, 4.27, 4.88), 6	4.09 (4.27 4.89), 4,000–5,600GVW
	3.31 (3.73, 4.09), V8	4.27 (4.88, 5.87), 6,600–7,600 GVW
		4.88 (5.87), 8,000–9,000 GVW

Dimensions and Capacities	Wagoneer	Truck
Wheelbase	110 in	120/126/132 in
Length x Width x Height	183.6 x 75.6 x 64.2 in	183.75 x 78.9 x 69.5 in 195.75 x 78.6 x 69.5 in 200.56 x 78.9 x 69.8 in
Curb Weight	3,806 lbs (I-6) 3,982 lbs (350 V8)	3,243 lbs (J-2000, I-6) 3,673 lbs (J-3000, V8) 4,367 lbs (J-4000, V8)
Gross Vehicle Weight	4,500 lbs	4,000, 5,000, 5,600, 6,000 lbs 6,600, 7,000, 7,600, 8,000 lbs 8,600, 9,000 lbs
Fuel Capacity	18 gal (1963-1967) 22 gal (1968-1970)	18 gal (1963-1968) 20 gal (1968-1970) 15 gal aux (opt 1970 camper spec)

Wagoneer, Grand Wagoneer, 1971–1991
J-Series Truck, 1971–1987

Engine	258 (1974)	304 (1974)	360 2-bbl/4-bbl (1974)
Type	6-cylinder OHV	V8 OHV	V8 OHV
Displacement	258 ci	304 ci	360 ci
Bore and Stroke	3.75x3.90 in	3.75x3.44 in	4.08x3.44 in
Compression Ratio	8.0:1	8.4:1	8.25:1
Power	110 hp @ 3,500 rpm	150 hp @ 4,200 rpm	175 hp @ 4,000 rpm/195 hp @ 4,000 rpm
Torque	195 ft-lbs @ 2,000 rpm	245 ft-lbs @ 2,500 rpm	285 ft-lbs @ 2,400/295 ft-lbs @ 2,900 rpm

Engine	401 (1974-1978)
Type	V8 OHV
Displacement	401 ci
Bore and Stroke	4.16x3.68 in
Compression Ratio	8.35:1
Power	215 hp @ 4,200 rpm
Torque	320 ft-lbs @ 2,800 rpm

Transmission		Manual	Automatic
Type and Model	1	3-speed Warner T-14A (1971-1979 6-cylinder Wagoneers)	3-speed GM TH-400 (1971-1979 with Quadra Trac)
	2	3-speed Warner T-15A (1971-1979 V8 Wagoneer and trucks)	3-speed Chrysler 727 (1980-1991 Wagoneer, 1980-87 truck)
	3	4-speed Warner T-18 (1971-1979 Wagoneer, 1971-87 trucks)	
	4	4-speed Tremec T-176 (1980-1986 Wagoneer and truck)	

Transfer Case		Part-Time	Full-Time
Type and Model	1	2-speed, Dana 20 (std, 1971-1979 manual trans)	1- or 2-speed, BW 1339 "Quadra-Trac" (1971-1979 automatic transmission)
	2	2-speed, NP-208 "Command-Trac" (std, 1980-1991)	2-speed, NP-219 "Quadra Trac" (opt, 1980-1985)
	3		2-speed, NP-229 "Selec Trac" (opt, 1983-1986)
	4		2-speed, NP-228 "Quadra-Trac" (opt, 1985-1991)
	5		2-speed, NP-242 "Selec-Trac" (opt, 1987-1991)

Axles	
Front Type and Model	FF, Dana 44
Rear Type and Model	SF, Dana 44 (1971-1975 Wag, 1/2-ton truck, 1974-1983 wide track, 1987-1991 Grand Wagoneer) SF, AMC-20 (1976-1986 Wagoneer and 1/2- ton truck) SF, Dana 60 (1971-1987 3/4 -ton truck) FF, Dana 60 (1971-1987, 3/4-ton, 1-ton truck)
Ratios (std/opt)	3.07, 3.31/ 3.54, 3.73 (Wagoneer) 3.07, 3.54/ 3.73, 4.09 (truck)

Dimensions and Capacities	Wagoneer	Truck
Wheelbase	109 in	119/131 in
Length x Width x Height	183.7 x 75.6 x 65.3 in	188.6/200.6 in
Curb Weight	4,221 lbs	3,993 lbs (1/2-ton)
Gross Vehicle Weight	5,600 lbs	5,200 lbs 6,500 lbs 7,200 lbs 8,000 lbs
Fuel Capacity	20.3 gal	19 gal

Jeepster Commando, Commando, 1967–1973

Engine	1967–1971 Std/Opt	1972–1973 std/opt
Type	4-cylinder F-head/V6 OHV	6-cylinder OHV/V8 OHV
Displacement	134.2 ci/225 ci	232 ci/258 ci/304 ci
Bore and Stroke	3.12x4.37 in/3.75x3.40 in	3.75x3.50 in/3.75x3.90 in/3.75x3.44 in
Compression Ratio	6.9:1/9.0:1	8.0:1/8.0:1/8.5:1
Power	75 hp @ 4,000 rpm/ 160 hp @ 4,200 rpm	100 hp @ 3,600 rpm /110 hp @ 3,500 rpm / 150 hp @ 4,200 rpm
Torque	114 ft-lbs @ 2,000 rpm / 235 ft-lbs @ 2,400 rpm	185 ft-lbs @ 1,800 rpm / 195 ft-lbs @ 2,000 rpm /245 ft-lbs @ 2,500 rpm

Transmission		1967–1971	1972–1973
Type and Model	1	3-speed, Warner T-90L (4-cylinder)	3-speed, Warner T-14A (I-6)
	2	3-speed, Warner T-14A (V6)	3-speed, Warner T-15A (V8)
	3	Auto, GM TH-400	4-speed, Warner T-18 (I-6)
	4		Auto, GM TH-400

Transfer Case	
Type and Model	2-speed, Spicer 20, all models

Axles	1967–1971	1972–1973
Front Type and Model	FF, Spicer 27AF	FF, Dana 30
Rear Type and Model	SF, Spicer 30 (1967-69 4 cylinder) SF, Spicer 44	SF, Dana 44
Ratios (std/opt)	3.31/3.73 automatic (V6) 3.73/4.27 or 4.88 manual (V6) 4.27/5.38 manual (F-4)	3.73/4.27 all

Dimensions and Capacities	1967–1971	1972–1973
Wheelbase	101 in	104 in
Length x Width x Height	168.4 x 65.2 x 62.4 in	174.5 x 65.2 x 62.4 in
Curb Weight	2,966 lbs (V6, SW)	3,010 lbs (I-6, SW)
Gross Vehicle Weight	3,550 lbs (std)/4,200 lbs (opt)	3,900 lbs (std)/4,700 lbs (opt)
Fuel Capacity	15 gal	16.5 gal

Cherokee XJ, 1984–1999
Comanche MJ, 1986–1992

Engine	4-cylinder (1990)	V6	4.0L six
Type	I-4 OHV	V-6 OHV	I-6 OHV
Displacement	151 ci	173 ci	241 ci
Bore and Stroke	3.88x3.19 in	3.50x2.99 in	3.88x3.14 in
Compression Ratio	9.2:1	8.5:1	8.8:1
Power	117 hp @ 5,000 rpm	115 hp @ 4,800 rpm	190 hp @ 4,750 rpm
Torque	135 ft-lbs @ 3,500 rpm	145 ft-lbs @ 2,400 rpm	225 ft-lbs @ 4,000 rpm

Transmission (XJ and MJ)

Type and Model	4-speed, Aisin Warner AX-4
	(1984–1987, mostly 4-cylinder)
	5-speed, Peugeot BA-10
	(1987–1989, mostly 4.0L 6-cylinder)
	5-speed, AisinWarner AX-5
	(1984–1994, mostly 4-cylinder)
	5-speed, Aisin Warner AX-15
	(1989–1999, 6-cylinder)
	3-speed automatic, Chrysler 904, 999
	(1984–1991, opt, V6 and mostly 4-cylinder)
	4-speed automatic, Aisin Warner AW30-40
	(1987–1991, opt, 6-cylinder)

Transfer Case

	XJ	MJ
Type and Model	2-speed, NP-207 (1984–1987)	2-speed, NP-208
	2-speed, NP-229 full-time	(1986–1987, std, 1986–1992, metric ton)
	2-speed, NP-231J	2-speed, NP-228 full-time (1986–1987)
	(1988–1999, later called NV-231J)	2-speed, NP-231J
	2-speed, NP-242 full-time	2-speed, NP-242 full-time (1988–1992)
	(1987–1999, later called NV-242)	

Axles

	XJ	MJ
Front Type and Model	FF, Dana 30	FF, Dana 30
Rear Type and Model	SF, Dana 35	SF, Dana 35
	SF, Dana 44 (opt, 1987)	SF, Dana 44 (1986–1992 metric ton)
Ratios (std/opt)	3.07/3.55 manual/ automatic 6-cylinder 3.07, 3.55/4.10, 4.56	
	(1984–1999)	
	4.11 manual 4-cylinder (1984–1999)	
	3.73 automatic 4-cylinder (1984–1996)	

Dimensions and Capacities

	XJ	MJ
Wheelbase	101.4 in	113 in (1987–1992 shortbed)
		119.9 in (1986–1992 longbed)
Length x Width x Height	167 x 70.5 x 63.2 in	179.2 x 71.7 x 63.7 in (shortbed)
		195.2 x 71.7 x 63.7 in (longbed)
Curb Weight	3,153 lbs (4dr, 6-cylinder)	2,914 lbs (shortbed)
		3,069 lbs (longbed)
Gross Vehicle Weight	4,900 lbs	4,001 lbs/6,000 lbs
Fuel Capacity	20.3 gal	16gal (shortbed)
		18 gal (longbed, opt shortbed)
		23.5 gal (opt longbed)

Grand Cherokee ZJ, 1993–1999
Grand Wagoneer ZJ, 1993

Engine	6-cylinder	V8 (1993–1998)	V8 (1999–on)
Type	I-6 OHV	V8 OHV	V8 OHV
Displacement	241 ci	318 cid/360 ci	287 ci
Bore and Stroke	3.88x3.41 in	3.91x3.31/4.00x3.58 in	3.66x3.40 in
Compression Ratio	8.8:1	8.9:1/8.7:1	9.3:1
Power	190 hp @ 4,600 rpm	220 hp @ 4,400 rpm/	235 hp @ 4,800 rpm
		245 hp @ 4,000 rpm	
Torque	220 ft-lbs @ 2,400 rpm	300 ft-lbs @ 3,200 rpm/	295 ft-lbs @ 3,200 rpm
		335 ft-lbs @ 2,800 rpm	

Transmission

Type and Model	4-speed automatic, AW-30-40, 6-cylinder (1992–early 1993)
	4-speed automatic, 42RE (6-cylinder early 1993–on)
	4-speed automatic, 46RH (V8, 1993–1995)
	4-speed automatic, 44RE (5.2L V8, 1996–on)
	4-speed automatic, 46RE (5.9L V8, 1998)
	5-speed automatic, 45RFE (4.7L V8, 1999–on)

Transfer Case

Type and Model	2-speed, NV-231J part time,"Command -Trac"(1993–1995)
	2-speed, NV-242 full-time, "Selec-Trac" (1993–on)
	2-speed, NV-249 full-time, "Quadra-Trac" (1996–on)
	2-speed, NV-247 full-time, "Quadra-Trac II" (1999–on)

Axles

Front Type and Model	FF, Dana 30
Rear Type and Model	SF, Dana 35 (1993)
	SF, Dana 44 (V8 models)
Ratios (std/opt)	3.54/3.73

Dimensions and Capacities

	ZJ	WJ
Wheelbase	105.9 in	105.9 in
Length x Width x Height	177.1 x 70.7 x 64.9 in	181.5 x 72.3 x 69.4 in
Curb Weight	4,261 lbs (V8)	4,050 lbs (V8)
Gross Vehicle Weight	5,500 lbs	5,500 lbs
Fuel Capacity	23 gal	20.5 gal

Willys 4x2 Station Wagons and Panel Deliveries, 1946–1965
Willys 4x2 Trucks, 1947–1951
Willys Jeepster, 1948–1951

Engine	4-63 Models	4-73/75 Models	6-63 Models
Type	4-cylinder L-head	4-cylinder F-head	6-cylinder L-head
Displacement	134.2 ci	134.2 ci	148.4 ci
Bore and Stroke	3.13x4.38 in	3.13x4.38 in	3.00x3.50 in
Compression Ratio	6.48:1 (7.1:1 opt)	6.9:1 (7.4:1 opt)	6.42:1
Power	63 hp @ 4,000 rpm	75 hp @ 4,000 rpm	70 hp @ 4,000 rpm
Torque	105 ft-lbs @ 2,000 rpm	114 ft-lbs @ 2,000 rpm	118 ft-lbs @ 1,600 rpm

Engine	6-73 Models	685 Models	6-226 Models
Type	6-cylinder L-head	6-cylinder F-head	6-cylinder L-head
Displacement	161 ci	161 ci	226.2 ci
Bore and Stroke	3.13x3.50 in	3.13x3.50 in	3.31x4.38 in
Compression Ratio	6.9:1	7.6:1 (8.1:1)	6.86:1 (7.3:1)
Power	75 hp @ 4,000 rpm	90 hp @ 4,000 rpm	115 hp @ 3,850 rpm
Torque	125 ft-lbs @ 2,000 rpm	135 ft-lbs @ 2,000 rpm	190 ft-lbs @ 1,800 rpm

Engine	6-230 Models
Type	6-cylinder OHC
Displacement	230 ci
Bore and Stroke	3.34x4.38 in
Compression Ratio	8.5:1 (7.5:1)
Power	140 hp @ 4,000 rpm (133 hp @ 4,000 rpm)
Torque	210 ft-lbs @ 1,750 rpm (199 ft-lbs @ 2,400 rpm)

Transmission	Wagon to 1955	Wagon after 1955	Truck
Type and Model	3-speed, Warner T-96/		3-speed, Warner T-90E
	3-speed, Warner T-86		

Axles	Wagons	Truck
Rear Type and Model	SF, Spicer 23-1	SF, Timken 51540
	SF, Spicer 44 (6-226)	SF, Spicer 41 (1947)
Ratios (std/opt)	5.38:1 (4-cylinder)	5.38:1/6.17:1
	4.88:1/5.38 (6-cylinder)	

Dimensions and Capacities	Wagons	Truck
Wheelbase	104 in (104.5 after 1955)	118 in
Length x Width x Height	176.25 x 68.81 x 72.75 in	182.5 x 73.16 x 74.5 in
Curb Weight	3,045 lbs (SW)	3,221 lbs (4-63 pickup)
	3,365 lbs (Panel)	
Gross Vehicle Weight	3,875 lbs (1947 4-63 SW)	4,700 lbs(4-63 HT)
		5,300 lbs (4-63)
Fuel Capacity	15 gal	15 gal

APPENDIX 3:
ENTHUSIAST DIRECTORY

Books and Literature

Army Motors
P. O. Box 520378
Independence, MO 64052
(800) 365-5798
The MVPA magazine with a lot of military jeep information.

Amazon Books
amazon.com
Huge internet bookseller with many Jeep titles.

Auto Book Center
(800) 448-6244
Jeep shop manuals.

Dyment Distribution Service
P. O. Box 360450
Strongsville, OH 44136
(216) 572-0725
Jeep literature.

Hemmings Motor News
P. O. Box 100, Rte. 9W
Bennington, VT 05201
(800) 227-4373
Huge monthly classified ad magazine, nationwide coverage.

MBI Publishing Co.
729 Prospect Avenue, P. O. Box 1
Osceola, WI 54020-0001
(800) 458-0454
Many Jeep titles.

Military Vehicles Magazine
12 Indian Head Road
Morristown, NJ 07960
(973) 285-0716
(973) 539-5934
MVehicle@aol.com
Bimonthy magazine with a lot of military jeep information.

Portrayal Press
P. O. Box 1190
Andover, NJ 07821
(973) 579-5781 phone/fax
www.portrayal.com
Huge variety of military and civilian manual, plus books and literature.

Walter Miller
6710 Brooklawn Parkway
Syracuse, NY 13211
(315) 432-8282
Original Jeep manuals and literature.

National Jeep Clubs and Groups

American Jeepster Club (1967–1973 Jeepsters)
P. O. Box 653
Lincoln, CA 95648-0653
Camp Jeep
(800) 789-JEEP

Colorado Full-Sized Jeep Association
www.cfsja.org/
(303) 699-6778

Forward Control Jeep Association
P. O. Box 343
Stevensville, MT 59870

Jeep Club of America
2909 Crystal Palace Lane
Pasadena, MD 21222

Middle Atlantic Four Wheel Drive Association
149 Dwight Avenue
Hillsdale, NJ 07642
www.ufwda.org/mafwda/

Midstates Jeepster Association
Dottie Wright, Editor
5905 N. 300 W.
Michigan City, IN 46360

Military Vehicle Preservation Association (MVPA)
P. O. Box 520378
Independence, MO 64052-0378
(800) 365-5798

The Willys Club
P. O. Box 5466
Plainfield, NJ 07060

United Four Wheel Drive Association
4505 W., 700 S.
Shelbyville, IN 46176
(800) 44-UFWDA
www.ufwda.com

West Coast Willys
Walt Mikolajcik, Editor
4000 Green Valley Road
Suisun, CA 94585

Willys-Overland Jeepster Club
Pete Mozzone, Editor
167 Worcester Street
Taunton, MA 02780-2088

Alabama

Rock Solid Jeep Club Alabama 4X4
1394 Downs Road
Mt. Olive, AL 35117
rocksolid.itgo.com

California

Napa Valley Jeepers
P.O. Box 2162
Napa, CA 94558
community.webtv.net/Trailbo/NapaValleyJeepers

Colorado

Grand Mesa Jeep Club
P. O. Box 4915
Grand Junction, CO 81502

Mile-Hi Jeep Club
P. O. Box 8293
Denver, CO 80201-8293
www.mhjc.org

Florida

Jeepers Jeep Club
669 SW Nichols Terrace
Port St. Lucie, FL 34953
www.jeepersjeepclub.com

White Sands Jeep Club
Pensacola Area
home.off-road.com/µwsjc

Georgia

Team Dixie 4x4
30 St. Ignatius Close
Alpharetta, GA 30022
www.homestead.com/southernjeeps

Illinois

Great Lakes Jeep Thing
c/o Don Birren
383 N. Colony
Round Lake Park, IL 60073
members.xoom/gljt/

Two Rivers Jeep Club
www.trjc.net
(630) 717-5337

Kansas

Flatlanders Jeep Club Manhattan, KS
P.O. Box 75
Ogden, KS 66517
www.jedi.com/flatlanders/

Maine

Overland Jeepers of Maine
P. O. Box 1167
Bethel, ME 04217
www.midcoast.com/µjeeps/index.html

Massachusetts

Bay State Jeepers
Shrewsbury, Massachusetts
members.tripod.com/Baystate_Jeepers/

Oregon

Jolly Jeepers
115 E. Arlinton
Gladstone, OR 97027
www.jollyjeepers.org

Oregon BushHackers
www.europa.com/%7Ebateman/obh/

Pennsylvania

PA Jeeps, Inc.
P.O. Box 3326
York, PA 17402-0326
www.pajeeps.org/

Texas

Jeeps of North Texas
P.O. Box 861506
Plano, TX 75086-1506
www.jeepn.com

INDEX